NEW CANADIAN PERSPECTIVES

Languages in Canada

1996 Census

Louise Marmen and Jean-Pierre Corbeil

D0910813

5

√

The opinions expressed in this publication are those of the authors and do not necessarily reflect federal government policy or opinion.

Canadian Cataloguing in Publication Data

Marmen, Louise

Languages in Canada : 1996 census

(New Canadian perspectives, ISSN 1203-8903)
Text in English and French on inverted pages.
Title on added t.p.: Les langues au Canada, recensement de 1996.
ISBN 0-662-64105-1
Cat. no. CH3-2-8/1999

1. Canada -- Languages -- Statistics.
2. English language -- Canada -- Statistics.
3. French language -- Canada -- Statistics.
4. Linguistic minorities -- Canada -- Statistics.
5. Linguistic demography -- Canada -- Statistics.
6. Canada -- Census, 1996.
I. Corbeil, Jean-Pierre, 1961-
II. Canada. Canadian Heritage.
III. Title.
IV. Series.

P119.32C3M37 1999   306.44'0971'021   C99-980110-4E

TABLE OF CONTENTS

PREFACE

This text is an updated version of a study published under the same title following the 1991 Census.[1] The text, tables and graphics have been adapted to reflect the new data from the 1996 Census. While seeking to remain true to the initial goal of presenting in a straightforward manner the country's basic demographic reality—certain analyses have been expanded.

The 1871 Census, undertaken a few years after the adoption of the country's Constitution, highlighted the ethnic duality of the population—61% of British origin and 31% of French origin. Eighty years later, following the Second World War, those of French origin still represented 31% of the population, while the British segment had declined to 48%. The stability of the proportion with French origin was due to their high fertility; the decline in those of British origin was due to the importance of international immigration in demographic growth in the years before and after the First World War. In 1951, 20% of the population had neither British nor French origins, a considerable increase since 1871 (nearly 8%)—those of aboriginal origin still represented about one percent of the population. The ethnic diversity of the population has been accentuated over the past half century by the high levels of international immigration and the gap between the fertility rates of the aboriginal population and that of other Canadians.

The growing number of inter-ethnic marriages has diminished the relevance of using statistical categories based on ethnic origin, at least for most of those in the population whose settlement goes back two or more generations. In fact, since the 60s, linguistic categories have been an increasing attractive and commonly used alternative. This is one reason that justifies using demolinguistic

---

[1]   Brain Harrison and Louise Marmen, *Languages in Canada*, Focus on Canada Series, Statistics Canada and Prentice Hall Inc., Catalogue No. 96-313E, 1994.

1

statistics to understand the situation of the two major groups in the country. The demolinguistic statistics have also had the advantage of being roughly comparable over the last half-century, which is not so for the statistics on ethnic origin.

Over the years, ethnic duality has given way to the linguistic duality. The two major ethnic groups represented more than 90% of the population in 1871; in 1996, 90% of the population speaks French or English most often in the home. However, this permanence masks the very different evolution experienced by English- and French-speaking communities across the country. It is precisely the objective of this text to examine the various factors and implications of this evolution.

Réjean Lachapelle
Director, Demography Division
Statistics Canada

INTRODUCTION

In Canada, two large official language groups represent about 83% of the population. There are also numerous other language groups, none of which represents more than three percent of Canadians. Both geography—5,500 km (3,400 miles) from coast to coast—and history play an important role in understanding the language situation.

Because they live in different parts of the country, many Anglophones have little contact with the French-speaking population and many Francophones would seldom encounter an Anglophone. Francophones are located mostly in Quebec and the neighbouring provinces of New Brunswick and Ontario. Only three percent of Francophones live in other provinces and territories. The location of the French mother tongue population reflects the early settlement of the French in New France and their low propensity to migrate to other provinces.

If we look at Canadians as a whole, we find that the language that most (84%) of them can speak is English, followed by French which about one-third (31%) of the population can speak. About one in six Canadians (17%) speak both official languages, according to the 1996 Census. Those who live in areas where the two language groups are in close proximity have a far greater tendency to speak both English and French. For example, half of the population in the Montreal metropolitan area and 44% of the population of Ottawa-Hull can speak the two official languages.

The Canadian population also shows a high level of linguistic diversity—20% are able to speak a language other than English or French. The fact that almost one in five Canadians can speak a non-official language is largely explained by the high proportion of immigrants in the country. In Canada, 17% of the population consists of immigrants, compared to 8% in the United States. Those able to speak a language other than English or French tend to be concentrated in large urban areas.

How has the language situation evolved in Canada over the last forty-five years? What factors determine the size of language groups in Canada and the tendency of languages to grow or decline? These are two of the principal questions dealt with in this analysis.

Chapter 1 covers the evolution of the English language in Canada between 1951 and 1996, including the size and distribution of the English mother tongue population, the use of English as home language, knowledge of English among the Canadian population as well as the use of English as first official language spoken. While the English mother tongue group grew considerably outside Quebec, the number and percentage of Anglophones in Quebec declined markedly between 1971 and 1996. Fewer than one Quebecer in ten (9%) reported their mother tongue as English at the time of the 1996 Census.

Chapter 2 examines changes in the French language group and the French language. While the number of Francophones increased considerably since 1951, the proportion of Canadians with French mother tongue declined. Outside Quebec, the proportion declined from 7% to 5%, though the number increased by 250,000. Chapter 3 explores the growth and decline of various non-official languages in Canada. Largely influenced by different waves of immigrants coming to the country, the language composition of this population has changed considerably since the 1950s.

Chapter 4 examines the growth in the number and percentage of Canadians who speak both official languages. English Canadians have a greater tendency to speak French than in the past. French Canadians, who have a much greater tendency to speak both languages than their Anglophone counterparts, also experienced growth in bilingualism. Another important topic related to language is also discussed in this chapter: the increase in numbers of Canadians who speak neither English nor French. Chapter 5 analyses the main factors which have contributed to changes in the language situation in Canada. The balance of these factors has changed markedly since 1951, with immigration playing a vital role in the most recent decade.

THE ENGLISH LANGUAGE

The 1996 Census showed that 24.0 million Canadians could speak English (84%), 19.3 million spoke English most often at home (68%) and 17.1 million had English mother tongue (60%).

English Mother Tongue

Mother tongue is defined here as the first language a person learned at home in childhood and still understood at the time of the census.

The percentage of the population which had English as its mother tongue (Anglophones) changed very little between 1951 and 1996. Since 1981, the figures have shown a slight decline in the percentage of Anglophones in Canada. Without the heavy immigration to Canada of many people with a language other than English or French as mother tongue, an increase in the proportion of Anglophones would have occurred.

In Quebec, the proportion of Anglophones has declined continuously, dropping from 14% in 1951 to 9% in 1996. This has resulted largely from the English mother tongue population leaving Quebec to live in other provinces, particularly during the 1970s.

While the proportion of Anglophones in Canada has changed very little since 1951, the number grew in each decade, more than doubling from 8.3 million in 1951 to 17.1 million in 1996. However, the pattern was very different in Quebec, where there was an increase of about 230,000 in the first two decades, followed by a decline of about 167,000 since then. As a result of this reversal, the net effect was only a slight increase in the number of Quebec Anglophones between 1951 and 1996.

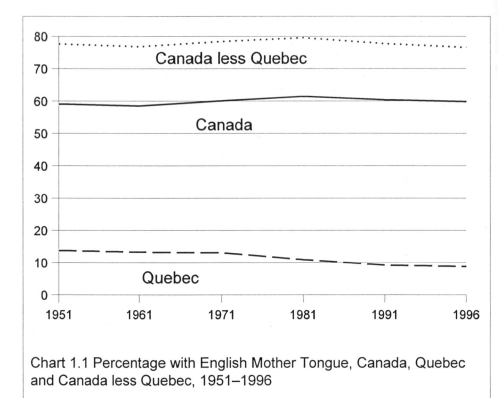

Chart 1.1 Percentage with English Mother Tongue, Canada, Quebec and Canada less Quebec, 1951–1996

Source: Appendix, table A.1.

Table 1.1 Population with English Mother Tongue, Canada, Quebec and Canada less Quebec, 1951–1996

	Canada		Quebec		Canada less Quebec	
	Numbers ('000)	%	Numbers ('000)	%	Numbers ('000)	%
1951	8,280.8	59.1	558.3	13.8	7,722.6	77.6
1961	10,660.5	58.5	697.4	13.3	9,963.1	76.8
1971	12,967.4	60.1	788.8	13.1	12,178.6	78.4
1981	14,784.8	61.4	693.6	10.9	14,091.2	79.5
1991	16,311.2	60.4	626.2	9.2	15,685.0	77.7
1996	17,072.4	59.8	621.9	8.8	16,450.6	76.6

Source: Appendix, table A.1.

Why did the number of Anglophones in Canada more than double between 1951 and 1996? The most rapid growth occurred during the 1950s and 1960s, when women of childbearing age had a much higher level of fertility than those in the two subsequent decades. The English mother tongue group also grew considerably through immigration. Of all the immigrants who settled in Canada between 1991 and 1996 (and who were still in Canada at the time of the 1996 Census), 17% had English as their mother tongue. In addition, the children of immigrants often learn English as mother tongue.

Between provinces, the percentage of Anglophones varies considerably. New Brunswick has a large proportion in each of the two official language groups (65% Anglophone and 33% Francophone), while Quebec is largely Francophone with the Anglophone population representing less than 9%. The three most eastern provinces have very high percentages of people whose mother tongue is English (more than 93%). Ontario and the western provinces, where more immigrants have settled, have larger populations with non-official languages as mother tongue. This accounts for the lower percentages of Anglophones.

Though the number of Anglophones increased in all provinces except Newfoundland and Quebec between 1991 and 1996, the proportion dropped in some provinces. The decline, slight in most cases, was largely attributable to the arrival of immigrants with a mother tongue other than English.

Table 1.2 Population with English Mother Tongue, Canada, Provinces, Territories and Canada less Quebec, 1991 and 1996

	1991		1996	
	Numbers ('000)	%	Numbers ('000)	%
Canada	16,311.2	60.4	17,072.4	59.8
Newfoundland	555.9	98.6	539.0	98.5
Prince Edward Island	120.8	94.3	125.0	94.1
Nova Scotia	831.6	93.3	838.3	93.2
New Brunswick	462.9	64.6	476.4	65.3
Quebec	626.2	9.2	621.9	8.8
Ontario	7,443.5	74.6	7,777.7	73.1
Manitoba	793.3	73.5	822.3	74.7
Saskatchewan	812.6	83.3	823.7	84.4
Alberta	2,045.9	81.2	2,175.8	81.5
British Columbia	2,562.2	78.9	2,809.4	76.1
Yukon	24.6	88.7	26.6	86.8
N.W.T.	31.7	55.2	36.3	56.7
Canada less Quebec	15,685.0	77.7	16,450.6	76.6

Source: Appendix, table A.1.

Canadians with an English mother tongue make up a very large percentage of the population in all provinces except Quebec and New Brunswick, and in the Northwest Territories. In Quebec, where those with English as their mother tongue comprise 9% of the population, almost three quarters live in the Montreal census metropolitan area (CMA). In New Brunswick, the English mother tongue population is concentrated in the southern part of the province, while in the Northwest Territories, Anglophones are concentrated in Yellowknife. Inuktitut is the mother tongue of about one third of the people living in the Northwest Territories.

English Home Language

Home language here refers to the language **most often** spoken at home at the time of the census.

Since 1971, Statistics Canada has collected data on the home language of Canadians. These data, when combined with the data on mother tongue, provide an indication of the degree to which various languages are growing or declining.

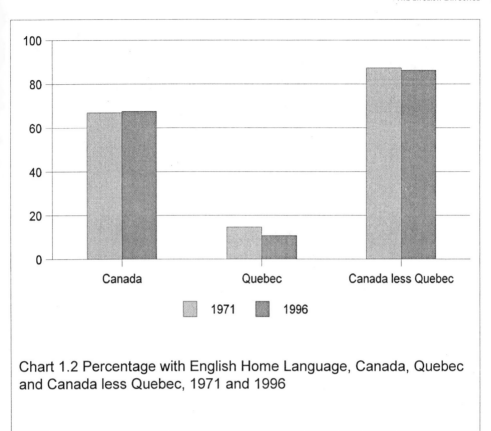

Chart 1.2 Percentage with English Home Language, Canada, Quebec and Canada less Quebec, 1971 and 1996

Source: Appendix, table A.2.

Results from the 1996 Census showed that for Canada as a whole, 68% of the population speaks English most often at home, compared to 11% in Quebec. Outside Quebec, almost nine out of ten Canadians speak English most often at home. The percentage of the Canadian population with English as its home language rose slightly, from 67% to 68% between 1971 and 1996. However, in Quebec, the proportion of the population with English as its home language declined from 15% to 11% over the same period. This decline is largely attributable to Anglophones leaving Quebec in the 1970s and 1980s.

In every province, there are more people with English as their home language than with English as their mother tongue, reflecting a shift toward English by people from other language groups.

The comparison of 1991 and 1996 data shows that the number of people with English as their home language rose in every province except Newfoundland. The percentage that speak English most often at home increased in New Brunswick, Manitoba, Saskatchewan and the Northwest Territories, while it decreased slightly or remained stable in the other provinces and the Yukon. In Ontario and British Columbia, the more significant decreases in the percentage were a result of immigration by people who speak non-official languages. This affects the proportion speaking English, since it increases the proportion that converses in other languages.

Table 1.3 Population with English Home Language, Canada, Provinces, Territories and Canada less Quebec, 1991 and 1996

	1991		1996	
	Numbers ('000)	%	Numbers ('000)	%
Canada	18 440.5	68.3	19 294.9	67.6
Newfoundland	559.5	99.2	542.6	99.2
Prince Edward Island	124.6	97.3	129.2	97.2
Nova Scotia	858.1	96.3	866.3	96.3
New Brunswick	488.6	68.2	502.5	68.9
Quebec	761.8	11.2	762.5	10.8
Ontario	8 499.5	85.2	8 900.8	83.6
Manitoba	947.1	87.7	971.6	88.3
Saskatchewan	921.1	94.4	923.4	94.6
Alberta	2 305.2	91.5	2 432.7	91.1
British Columbia	2 909.9	89.6	3 189.9	86.5
Yukon	26.7	96.7	29.2	95.4
N.W.T.	38.4	66.8	44.1	68.8
Canada less Quebec	17 678.7	87.6	18 532.4	86.3

Source: Appendix, table A.2.

Knowledge of English

In the census, knowledge of English and/or French was determined by a question about the ability to conduct a conversation in one or both languages. It should be noted that this question measured language knowledge rather than actual use of language.

While about 17% of the population of Canada speaks both English and French, most Canadians speak only one or the other. Some, mostly immigrants, speak neither of the official languages. The percentage of the population able to speak English grew between 1951 and 1996 both inside and outside Quebec. In 1996, 98% of people living outside Quebec and 43% of Quebecers were able to conduct a conversation in English.

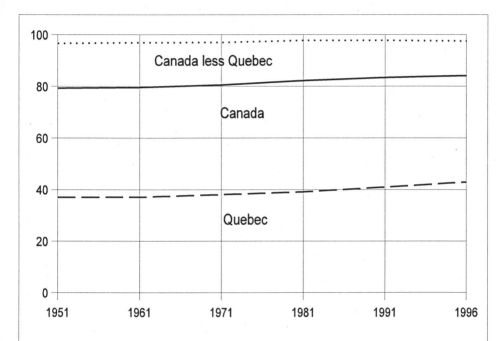

Chart 1.3 Knowledge of English, Canada, Quebec and Canada less Quebec, 1951–1996

Source: Appendix, table A.3.

Both the number and the percentage of Canadians able to speak English rose between 1991 and 1996. During this five-year period, numbers of English speakers increased in all provinces except Newfoundland (where there was a 3% decrease in the size of the provincial population), and the percentages able to conduct a conversation in English increased in Prince Edward Island, Newfoundland, New Brunswick, Quebec, Manitoba, Saskatchewan and the Northwest Territories. Declines in percentages of English speakers in the populations of Ontario and British Columbia were largely due to the arrival of new immigrants who were unable to speak English. Despite this decline, the number of English speakers in each of the provinces actually increased. The most significant increase was in Ontario, home of 43% of Canada's English-speaking population—where 621,000 English speakers joined the population in the five-year period.

Table 1.4 Population Able to Speak English, Canada, Provinces, Territories and Canada less Quebec, 1991 and 1996

	1991		1996	
	Numbers ('000)	%	Numbers ('000)	%
Canada	22,505.4	83.4	23,975.6	84.0
Newfoundland	562.9	99.8	546.4	99.9
Prince Edward Island	127.7	99.7	132.7	99.9
Nova Scotia	888.3	99.7	897.3	99.7
New Brunswick	626.5	87.4	655.7	89.9
Quebec	2,786.7	40.9	3,019.1	42.9
Ontario	9,729.9	97.5	10,351.1	97.3
Manitoba	1,063.9	98.6	1,087.0	98.8
Saskatchewan	969.9	99.4	971.3	99.5
Alberta	2,486.1	98.7	2,633.6	98.7
British Columbia	3,183.5	98.0	3,590.9	97.3
Yukon	27.6	99.8	30.6	99.7
N.W.T.	52.4	91.2	59.9	93.4
Canada less Quebec	19,718.7	97.7	20,956.5	97.6

Source: Calculated from Appendix, table A.3.

English first official language spoken

The first official language spoken represents the official language actually spoken which, in most cases, was acquired first. The data on first official language spoken are derived from the responses to the question on the knowledge of official languages, mother tongue and the language spoken in the home. In this way the Canadian population is sub-divided into four categories, English, French, English and French, and neither English nor French.

In 1996, 21.0 million Canadians had English as their first official language spoken. Approximately 91% of them could conduct a conversation in English but not in French. Nearly all of the rest of sub-population was made up of English-French bilinguals for whom English took precedence over French according to the information provided by the responses to the questions on mother tongue and language spoken in the home.

Persons having English as their first official language spoken represented 74% of the Canadian population. Outside Quebec, they represented more than 90% of the population in every province and territory except New Brunswick where they represented two-thirds of the population. In Quebec, English was the first official language spoken of 13% of the population.

In every province and territory the number of persons with English as their first official language spoken was greater than the number having this language as their mother tongue. Even in Quebec, where English is the minority official language, the same trend existed given the attraction of English among Allophones.

The number of persons with English as their first official language exceed the number which used this language most often in the home except in the Maritime provinces. In these three provinces, where there are few Allophones, Francophones accounted for most transfers towards English (language spoken most often in the home). These people have by definition French as their first official language since in deriving this variable mother tongue takes precedence over the language spoken most often in the home.

Table 1.5 Population with English as First Official Language Spoken, Mother Tongue or Home Language, Canada, Provinces, Territories and Canada less Quebec, 1996

	English					
	First Official Language Spoken[1]		Mother Tongue		Home Language	
	('000)	%	('000)	%	('000)	%
Canada	21,048.9	73.8	17,072.4	59.8	19,294.9	67.6
Newfoundland	544.4	99.5	53,9.1	98.5	542.6	99.2
P.E.I.	127.5	96.0	125.0	94.1	129.2	97.2
Nova Scotia	864.2	96.0	838.3	93.1	866.3	96.3
New Brunswick	488.2	66.9	476.4	65.3	502.5	68.9
Quebec	925.8	13.1	621.9	8.8	762.5	10.8
Ontario	9,891.9	92.9	7,777.7	73.1	8,900.8	83.6
Manitoba	1,042.2	94.7	822.3	74.7	971.6	88.3
Saskatchewan	954.2	97.7	823.7	84.3	923.4	94.6
Alberta	2,583.8	96.8	2,175.8	81.5	2,432.7	91.1
B.C.	3,538.5	95.9	2,809.4	76.1	3,189.9	86.5
Yukon	29.5	96.2	26.6	86.8	29.2	95.4
N.W.T.	58.6	91.4	36.3	56.6	44.1	68.8
Canada less Quebec	20,123.1	93.7	16,450.6	76.6	18,532.4	86.3

Source: 1996 Census of Canada, unpublished tabulations.

---

1.   Those in the English/French category have been allocated equally to the English category and the French category in order to improve the comparability of the data relating to mother tongue and home language.

THE FRENCH LANGUAGE

The 1996 Census showed that 8.9 million Canadians could conduct a conversation in French (31%), 6.4 million spoke French most often at home (23%) and 6.7 million had French as their mother tongue (24%).

French Mother Tongue

Although the number of people with French as their mother tongue (Francophones) has continued to increase in Canada, their proportion has declined over the last forty-five years. Between 1951 and 1996, the number of Francophones rose from 4.1 million to 6.7 million, but the proportion of Francophones in the population fell from 29% to 24%.

The proportional decline is largely explained by the heavy immigration of people whose mother tongue was a language other than French. For example, of the 1,039,000 immigrants enumerated in the 1996 Census as having arrived in Canada over the previous five years, only 3% had French as a mother tongue.

In the past, the high fertility rate of Francophone women in Canada offset the impact of immigration from other countries on the distribution of language groups. With a fertility higher than that of Anglophones, Francophones made up a steady 30% or so of the Canadian population for many years. Since the 1960s, though, the fertility rate of Francophone Canadian women has declined, so much so that their fertility level has become lower than that of Anglophone Canadian women since the seventies.

Outside Quebec, children of parents with a French mother tongue sometimes learn English rather than French in early childhood. The transmission of French mother tongue is not assured, particularly when one of the parents has English as a mother tongue. The size and proportion of the Francophone population are affected by this phenomenon.

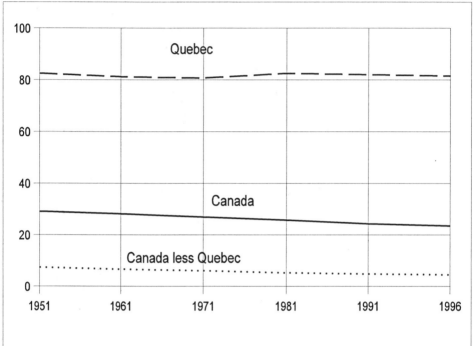

Chart 2.1 Percentage with French Mother Tongue, Canada, Quebec and Canada less Quebec, 1951–1996

Source: Appendix, table A.1.

Quebec is the only province in which the majority of the population has French as its mother tongue. In 1996, 86% of Francophones in Canada lived in Quebec. They accounted for 82% of the Quebec population. Although their number rose from 3.3 million in 1951 to 5.7 million in 1996, their proportion changed very little during that time. After decreasing between 1951 and 1971 due to both the decrease in the fertility of Francophone women and heavy immigration, the proportion of Francophones has reverted to the 1951 level since the 1980s. The proportion of Francophones rose as Anglophones left Quebec and moved to other provinces.

Outside Quebec, the Francophone population grew by 250,000 between 1951 and 1996, but the proportion of Francophones continuously declined.

Table 2.1 Population with French Mother Tongue, Canada, Quebec and Canada less Quebec, 1951–1996

	Canada		Quebec		Canada less Quebec	
	Numbers ('000)	%	Numbers ('000)	%	Numbers ('000)	%
1951	4,068.8	29.0	3,347.0	82.5	721.8	7.3
1961	5,123.2	28.1	4,269.7	81.2	853.5	6.6
1971	5,792.7	26.9	4,866.4	80.7	926.3	6.0
1981	6,177.8	25.7	5,254.2	82.5	923.6	5.2
1991	6,562.1	24.3	5,585.6	82.0	976.4	4.8
1996	6,711.6	23.5	5,741.4	81.5	970.2	4.5

Source: Appendix, table A.1.

The situation of Francophones varies widely from province to province. Quebec is the province with the highest proportion of persons whose mother tongue is French, followed by New Brunswick. It is in the latter province and in Ontario that more than three quarters (76%) of Francophones living outside Quebec are found. Since its entry into Confederation in 1949, Newfoundland's provincial population has always had the smallest proportion and lowest number of Francophones.

Between 1991 and 1996, the population with French as its mother tongue and the proportion of the Canadian population made up by that group has fallen in all provinces, except Quebec and British Columbia. In these two provinces, the number of Francophones has grown while their proportion has decreased. Only in the Yukon has both the number and the proportion of Francophones in the population increased.

17

Table 2.2 Population with French Mother Tongue, Canada, Provinces, Territories and Canada less Quebec, 1991 and 1996

	1991		1996	
	Numbers ('000)	%	Numbers ('000)	%
Canada	6,562.1	24.3	6,711.6	23.5
Newfoundland	2.9	0.5	2.4	0.4
Prince Edward Island	5.7	4.5	5.7	4.3
Nova Scotia	37.5	4.2	36.3	4.0
New Brunswick	243.7	34.0	242.4	33.2
Quebec	5,585.6	82.0	5,741.4	81.5
Ontario	503.3	5.0	499.7	4.7
Manitoba	50.8	4.7	49.1	4.5
Saskatchewan	21.8	2.2	19.9	2.0
Alberta	56.7	2.3	55.3	2.0
British Columbia	51.6	1.6	56.8	1.5
Yukon	0.9	3.3	1.2	3.8
N.W.T.	1.5	2.5	1.4	2.2
Canada less Quebec	976.4	4.8	970.2	4.5

Source: Appendix, table A.1.

French Home Language

The number of Canadians who speak French most often at home is growing: there were 6.4 million in 1996, compared with 5.5 million in 1971. However, the relative importance of French home language in the country as a whole has decreased, falling from 26% in 1971 to 23% in 1996. In Quebec, the number and proportion of persons with French as a home language increased between 1971 and 1996, while the situation was the reverse in the rest of Canada.

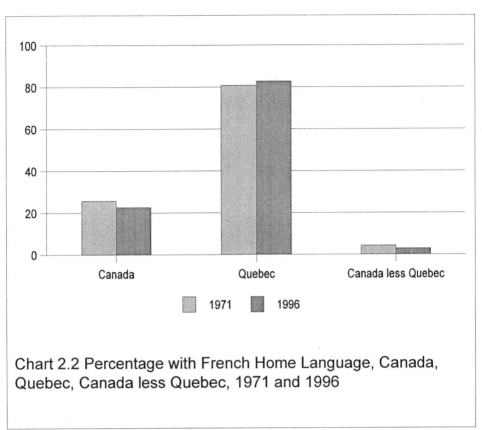

Chart 2.2 Percentage with French Home Language, Canada, Quebec, Canada less Quebec, 1971 and 1996

Source: Appendix, table A.2.

In all provinces and territories except Quebec, the number of persons with French as a mother tongue was greater than the number of persons with French as a home language. Thus, in the provinces of Saskatchewan, Alberta and British Columbia, more than three times as many people reported having French as a mother tongue than reported French as a home language in 1996. In Newfoundland, Manitoba, and the territories, less than half of the Francophones spoke French most often at home. In the other provinces, the fraction speaking French most often at home was higher. It is really only in New Brunswick that the vast majority of Francophones seem to retain their mother tongue as their home language. In 1996, 33% of the population of New Brunswick had French as a mother tongue and 30% had French as a home language. These persons lived mainly in the northern and eastern parts of the province.

In Quebec, French, the mother tongue of the majority, is likely to be spoken most often at home by Francophones, but also by certain persons in other language groups. Thus, in 1996 the proportion of Quebecers who spoke French most often at home (83%) was larger than that of Quebecers who reported French as mother tongue (82%).

Comparing the situation for French as a home language in 1991 and 1996 reveals a decrease in the number and proportion of people with French as a home language in almost all provinces and territories. Only the Yukon showed an increase in both; Quebec and British Columbia registered an increase in the number only.

Table 2.3 Population with French Home Language, Canada, Provinces, Territories and Canada less Quebec, 1991 and 1996

	1991		1996	
	Numbers ('000)	%	Numbers ('000)	%
Canada	6,288.4	23.3	6,448.6	22.6
Newfoundland	1.3	0.2	1.0	0.2
Prince Edward Island	3.0	2.4	3.0	2.3
Nova Scotia	22.3	2.5	20.7	2.3
New Brunswick	223.3	31.2	222.4	30.5
Quebec	5,651.8	83.0	5,830.1	82.8
Ontario	318.7	3.2	306.8	2.9
Manitoba	25.0	2.3	23.1	2.1
Saskatchewan	7.2	0.7	5.8	0.6
Alberta	20.2	0.8	17.8	0.7
British Columbia	14.6	0.4	16.6	0.4
Yukon	0.4	1.4	0.5	1.8
N.W.T.	0.7	1.2	0.6	1.0
Canada less Quebec	636.6	3.2	618.5	2.9

Source: Appendix, table A.2.

Knowledge of French

Despite the decline in the proportion of persons with French as a mother tongue or home language, the proportion of French speakers remained fairly stable (around 32%) between 1951 and 1996. The number of persons able to conduct a conversation in French nearly doubled during this period, rising from 4.5 million to 8.9 million. In Quebec, as well as in the other provinces and territories, except Saskatchewan, the proportion and number of persons in the population who know French has grown continuously since 1961.

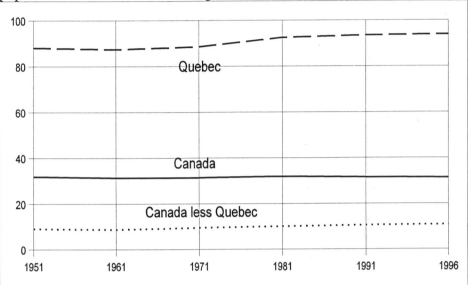

Chart 2.3 Knowledge of French, Canada, Quebec and Canada less Quebec, 1951–1996

Source: Appendix, table A.3.

Persons who know French are concentrated in Quebec. In 1996, some 75% of them lived in that province. However, since 1961 the concentration has declined. The decline is attributed to the increase in bilingualism among non-Francophones and has occurred despite the marked increase in the number of French speakers in the Quebec population. Over twenty-five years - that is, between 1971 and 1996 - the proportion of the population outside Quebec able to speak French among people with a mother tongue other than French rose from 4% to 7%. The popularity of second-language programmes (immersion or regular courses) in English-language schools has contributed to this increase.

In all provinces, except Saskatchewan, an increase was observed in the number and proportion of persons able to conduct a conversation in French between 1991 and 1996.

Table 2.4 Population Able to Speak French, Canada, Provinces, Territories and Canada less Quebec, 1991 and 1996

	1991		1996	
	Numbers ('000)	%	Numbers ('000)	%
Canada	8,509.0	31.5	8,920.4	31.3
Newfoundland	18.7	3.3	21.4	3.9
Prince Edward Island	13.2	10.3	14.7	11.1
Nova Scotia	78.0	8.8	85.4	9.5
New Brunswick	301.0	42.0	311.2	42.6
Quebec	6,371.9	93.6	6,612.3	93.9
Ontario	1,190.5	11.9	1,281.8	12.0
Manitoba	100.7	9.3	104.6	9.5
Saskatchewan	51.2	5.3	51.1	5.2
Alberta	169.1	6.7	180.1	6.8
British Columbia	208.3	6.4	250.4	6.8
Yukon	2.6	9.4	3.3	10.6
N.W.T.	3.6	6.2	4.1	6.4
Canada less Quebec	2,137.0	10.6	2,308.1	10.7

Source: Calculated from Appendix, table A.3.

French First Official Language Spoken

In 1996, 7.0 million Canadians had French as their first official language spoken. Approximately 58% could conduct a conversation in French, but not in English. Nearly all of the rest of this sub-population was made up of English-French bilinguals for whom French took precedence over English according to the information provided by the responses to the questions on mother tongue and language spoken in the home.

Persons with French as their first official language represented 25% of the Canadian population. In Quebec, where French is the mother tongue of the majority, it represented 86% of the population. In the other provinces and territories less than 5% of the population had French as their first official language, except in New Brunswick where the proportion reached 33%.

When French is spoken as a minority language the number of those with French as a first official language spoken is much closer to that of mother tongue than home language, which is always weaker. Furthermore, the number of persons with French as a mother tongue is generally slightly higher than the number with French as first official language spoken, since it excludes persons with French as a mother tongue but who are unable to conduct a conversation in their first language learned. This phenomenon is however counterbalanced in Ontario by Allophones with French as their first official language. The observed difference which favours first official language spoken is also explained by the decision to allocate half of the French and English category, which is made up principally of English-French bilinguals who have a non-official language as mother tongue and home language.

In Quebec, the number of persons with French as first official language spoken is much greater that those with French as mother tongue or those with French as home language. This is due to the large number of mother tongue and home language Allophones who are able to conduct a conversation in French but not in English.

Table 2.5 Population with French as First Official Language Spoken, Mother Tongue or Home Language, Canada, Provinces, Territories and Canada less Quebec, 1996

	French					
	First Official Language Spoken[1]		Mother Tongue		Home Language	
	('000)	%	('000)	%	('000)	%
Canada	7,018,055	24.6	6,711,645	23.5	6,448,605	22.6
Newfoundland	2,278	0.4	2,440	0.4	1,020	0.1
P.E.I.	5,330	4.0	5,720	4.3	3,045	2.3
Nova Scotia	34,610	3.8	36,310	4.0	20,710	2.3
N.B.	241,043	33.0	242,410	33.2	222,440	30.1
Quebec	6,047,405	85.8	5,741,440	81.5	5,830,080	82.8
Ontario	511,800	4.8	499,690	4.7	306,790	2.9
Manitoba	46,575	4.2	49,100	4.5	23,135	2.1
Saskatchewan	17,715	1.8	19,900	2.0	5,830	0.6
Alberta	52,500	2.0	55,290	2.0	17,820	0.6
B.C.	56,305	1.5	56,755	1.5	16,585	0.4
Yukon	1,115	3.6	1,170	3.8	545	1.8
N.W.T.	1,375	2.1	1,420	2.2	605	0.9
Canada less Quebec	970,650	4.5	970,205	4.5	618,520	2.9

Source: 1996 Census of Canada, unpublished tabulations.

[1] Those in the English/French category have been allocated equally to the English category and the French category in order to improve the comparability of the data relating to mother tongue and home language.

THE NON-OFFICIAL LANGUAGES

The presence of languages other than English or French in Canada reflects the ethnic and linguistic diversity that characterizes the nation. The 1996 Census showed that 5.8 million people (20%) could speak at least one language other than English or French, some 2.8 million (10%) spoke a non-official language most often at home and 4.7 million (17%) had a non-official language as mother tongue.

Mother Tongues Other than English or French

The percentage of the population with a non-official language as mother tongue rose between 1951 and 1996, largely because of an increase in the number of immigrants during this period, coupled with an increase in the tendency of immigrants to come from countries where languages other than English or French are spoken.

In Canada, the percentage of the population with a non-official language as mother tongue rose from 12% in 1951 to 17% in 1996. Outside Quebec, people with a non-official language as mother tongue represented 19% of the population in 1996, up from 15% in 1951. In Quebec, the presence of non-official languages changed considerably over this period, rising from 4% of the population in 1951 to 10% in 1996.

The number of Allophones (people with a language other than English or French as mother tongue) in Canada rose considerably between 1951 and 1996. From 1.7 million in 1951, the number has grown continually since then. This was most notable during the 1950s when a large number of immigrants from European countries made their way to Canada; over the last fifteen years,

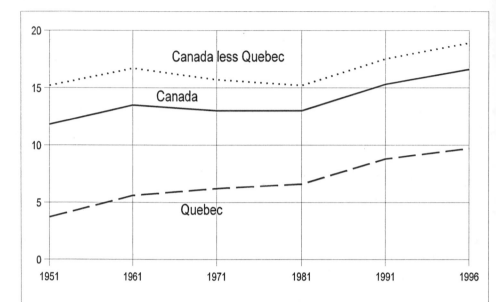

Chart 3.1 Percentage of the Population with Mother Tongue Other than English or French, Canada, Quebec and Canada less Quebec, 1951–1996

Source: Appendix, table A.1.

Table 3.1 Population with Mother Tongue Other than English or French, Canada, Quebec and Canada less Quebec, 1951–1996

	Canada		Quebec		Canada less Quebec	
	Numbers ('000)	%	Numbers ('000)	%	Numbers ('000)	%
1951	1,659.8	11.8	150.4	3.7	1,509.4	15.2
1961	2,454.6	13.5	292.1	5.6	2,162.4	16.7
1971	2,808.2	13.0	372.5	6.2	2,435.6	15.7
1981	3,120.9	13.0	421.3	6.6	2,699.6	15.2
1991	4,120.8	15.3	598.5	8.8	3,522.3	17.5
1996	4,744.1	16.6	681.8	9.7	4,062.3	18.9

Source: Appendix, table A.1.

immigration from Asia and the Caribbean has been a major catalyst for linguistic diversity. In Quebec, the number of people with a non-official language as mother tongue rose from 150,000 to 682,000 between 1951 and 1996. Outside Quebec, the number rose from 1.5 million to 4.1 million over the same period.

Between 1991 and 1996, the number of people with a non-official language as mother tongue rose in every province except Manitoba and Saskatchewan. The largest increase was in Ontario, where the number of people with a mother tongue other than English or French rose by 335,000, to represent 22% of the population (2.4 million people). Much of the increase resulted from the arrival of new immigrants in Toronto. In terms of average annual growth, the number of Allophones grew over the last five years by 67,000 compared to 57,000 during the 1981–91 period. However, in British Columbia—particularly Vancouver—the average annual growth was even greater: 38,000 over the last five years compared to 19,000 in the 1981 to 1991 period. Over the last five years the number of persons with a mother tongue other than French or English grew by the same number as it did during the entire 1981–1991 decade (190,000).

The percentage of the population with a non-official language as mother tongue declined in Manitoba and Saskatchewan, where German and Ukrainian groups have formed the bulk of non-official language groups in the past. Conversely, the percentage has increased in provinces that have received more recent immigrants, particularly in Ontario, Quebec and British Columbia.

Interestingly, those with a non-official language as mother tongue form only a very small percentage of the population in the eastern provinces. In fact, only a small percentage of immigrants to Canada take up residence east of Montreal. The location of people with a non-official language as mother tongue is largely a reflection of regional trends in terms of immigration.

Quebec has only a small percentage of its population (10% in 1996), with a non-official language as mother tongue compared with other large provinces. This reflects the traditional pattern of a disproportionate number of immigrants settling outside Quebec. While almost a quarter of Canada's population is located in Quebec, only 13% of immigrants are living there, according to the 1996 Census.

Table 3.2 Population with Mother Tongue Other than English or French, Canada, Provinces, Territories and Canada less Quebec, 1991 and 1996

	1991		1996	
	Numbers ('000)	%	Numbers ('000)	%
Canada	4,120.8	15.3	4,744.1	16.6
Newfoundland	5.1	0.9	5.7	1.0
Prince Edward Island	1.6	1.2	2.1	1.6
Nova Scotia	21.8	2.5	25.4	2.8
New Brunswick	9.9	1.4	10.8	1.5
Quebec	598.5	8.8	681.8	9.7
Ontario	2,030.2	20.3	2,365.4	22.2
Manitoba	235.3	21.8	228.9	20.8
Saskatchewan	141.6	14.5	133.0	13.6
Alberta	416.6	16.5	438.1	16.4
British Columbia	633.7	19.5	823.6	22.3
Yukon	2.2	8.0	2.9	9.4
N.W.T.	24.3	42.3	26.4	41.1
Canada less Quebec	3,522.3	17.5	4,062.3	18.9

Source: Appendix, table A.1.

The percentage of the population with a mother tongue other than English or French varies considerably from one census metropolitan area (CMA) to another; of Canada's 25 CMAs, Toronto had the largest proportion (37%), followed by Vancouver (34%) and Montreal (18%). Almost 60% of the population that reported having a non-official language as mother tongue lived in Toronto, Vancouver or Montreal.

Table 3.3 Population with Mother Tongue Other than English or French, Census Metropolitan Areas, 1996

Census Metropolitan Areas	1996	
	Number ('000)	Percentage
Calgary	152.0	18.6
Chicoutimi–Jonquière	0.7	0.4
Edmonton	167.2	19.6
Halifax	14.1	4.3
Hamilton	121.8	19.7
Kitchener	76.1	20.1
London	60.6	15.4
Montréal	602.9	18.3
Oshawa	28.0	10.5
Ottawa–Hull	137.6	13.8
Québec	11.7	1.8
Regina	20.9	10.9
Saint John (N.–B.)	2.0	1.6
Saskatoon	28.8	13.3
Sherbrooke	4.2	2.9
St. Catharines–Niagara	54.2	14.7
St. John's (Nfld.)	2.6	1.5
Sudbury	13.7	8.6
Thunder Bay	19.2	15.4
Toronto	1,565.9	37.0
Trois–Rivières	1.3	0.9
Vancouver	607.7	33.5
Victoria	33.5	11.2
Windsor	54.1	19.6
Winnipeg	132.4	20.1

Source: 1996 Census of Canada.

The sizes of language groups other than English or French reflect the most recent immigration trends. The ranking of the non-official languages reported most frequently as mother tongue in Canada have changed considerably over the years. In 1971, German was the most frequently reported non-official mother tongue among Canadians (559,000), with those reporting Italian as a close second (539,000). The German mother tongue group has since declined in numbers to 491,000 people in 1991 and to 471,000 in 1996, now only third in the list of languages. Over the same period, the Ukrainian mother tongue group has recorded the largest decrease in numbers (a 44% decrease), slipping from third in 1971 to eighth twenty-five years later. In 1996, 47% of people with Ukrainian mother tongue were aged 65 and over, compared to 12% for the overall Canadian population.

The Italian mother tongue group, which recorded a large increase between 1951 and 1971 (from 92,000 to 539,000) due to considerable immigration from Italy, has been declining ever since, to 514,000 in 1996. In contrast, the Chinese mother tongue group has been experiencing rapid growth in the last fifteen years, due to increased immigration during this period. Between 1991 and 1996, the number of people who reported Chinese as mother tongue increased 42% to 736,000, while during the twenty years before that five-year period, their number had grown in a fashion similar to the Italian group between 1951 and 1971. However, if the average annual growth of the two language groups during these twenty year periods was about the same (more than 21,000), there has been a remarkable average annual growth of the Chinese language group over the last five years. While the census metropolitan regions of Toronto and Vancouver accounted for 87% of all mother tongue Chinese persons during this five year period and they both experienced an average annual growth of about 18,000 persons from this group. Proportionately Vancouver experienced a greater increase. The percentage increase in this group was 65%, compared to 43% in Toronto.

Table 3.4 The Ten Largest Allophone (Mother Tongue) Groups, Canada, 1971, 1991 and 1996

Rank	1971		1991		1996	
1	German	559,0	Italian	538,7	Chinese	736,0
2	Italian	538,8	Chinese	516,9	Italian	514,4
3	Ukrainian	309,9	German	490,6	German	470,5
4	Dutch[1]	146,7	Portuguese	220,6	Spanish	228,6
5	Polish	136,5	Ukrainian	201,3	Portuguese	222,9
6	Greek	103,7	Polish	200,4	Polish	222,4
7	Chinese	95,9	Spanish	187,6	Punjabi	214,5
8	Hungarian	87,5	Punjabi	147,3	Ukrainian	174,8
9	Portuguese	85,8	Dutch	146,4	Arabic	166,2
10	Croatian, Serbian, etc,	75,6	Greek	133,0	Tagalog (Pilipino)	158,2

Sources : Census of Canada, 1971,1991 and 1996.

Other language groups that appear on the list of the largest Allophone groups in 1996 have also grown because of immigration. Thus, the Spanish, Portuguese, Punjabi, Arabic and Tagalog groups grew considerably in the twenty-five-year period leading up to 1996. Between 1991 and 1996 alone, the number of people who reported Punjabi, Arabic, Tagalog and Spanish as their mother tongue increased 46%, 39%, 36% and 22% respectively, while those reporting Portuguese increased only 1%. The Polish group, which has also increased its numbers markedly from 1971 to 1991 (a 47% increase), principally due to immigration during the 1980s, recorded a slowdown of its growth over the last five-year period, to 11%.

[1.] In 1971, Dutch includes respondents who reported Flemish or Frisian.

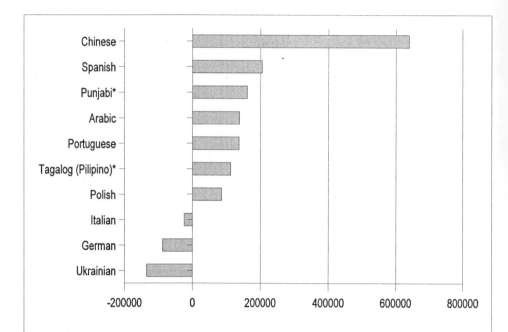

Chart 3.2 Change in Size of the 10 Largest Allophone Groups, Canada, 1971–1996

*No data available for Punjabi and Tagalog in 1971. Data from the 1981 Census where used for these languages.

Sources : Census of Canada,1971, 1981, and 1996.

Aboriginal Languages

The aboriginal languages have been spoken in Canada for a long time. Because of the concentration of various aboriginal groups in particular parts of the country, their presence is much more apparent in some provinces than in others. Cree is by far the most frequently reported mother tongue among the aboriginal languages (88,000), followed by Inuktitut (28,000), and Ojibway (26,000)

Except for people with Micmac mother tongue in Nova Scotia and New Brunswick, there are few aboriginal languages reported as mother tongue in the Atlantic provinces. Nova Scotia has the highest number, with 4,200 people reporting an aboriginal mother tongue. Those with an aboriginal language as mother tongue account for a sizeable proportion of the non-official languages in both Manitoba (17%) and Saskatchewan (25%). People with Cree as mother tongue are located in all provinces from Quebec to British Columbia, but are heavily concentrated in Manitoba and Saskatchewan (58%). The Ojibway mother tongue population is largely found in Ontario and Manitoba (89%), while 97% of those with Inuktitut as mother tongue live in the Northwest Territories or Quebec.

Table 3.5 The Most Frequently Reported Aboriginal Languages as Mother Tongues, Canada, 1996[1]

	Number	Principal concentration
Cree	87 550	Manitoba and Saskatchewan (58%)
Inuktitut	27 785	Northwest Territories and Quebec (97%)
Ojibway	25 885	Ontario and Manitoba (91%)
Montagnais–Naskapi	9 070	Quebec (86%)
Dene	9 005	Saskatchewan (77%)
Micmac	7 310	Nova Scotia and N.B. (85%)
Oji-Cree	5 395	Ontario (90%)
Dakota/Sioux	4 285	Alberta (70%)
Others	32 340	
Total	208 625	

Includes both single and multiple responses.
Source: 1996 Census of Canada.

Home Language Other than English or French

The number of people who speak a non-official language most often at home is growing in Canada, from 1.6 million in 1971 to 2.8 million in 1996. The proportion of the population with a non-official home language has also increased over this period, from 7% to 10%. This holds true for Quebec as well as for the other provinces and territories combined.

---

1.   On some Indian reserves and Indian settlements in the 1996 Census, enumeration was not permitted, or was interrupted before it could be completed. Moreover, some Indian reserves and Indian settlements were enumerated late or the quality of the collected data was considered inadequate. The impact of this under enumeration may be significant for some language groups, particularly those with small numbers.

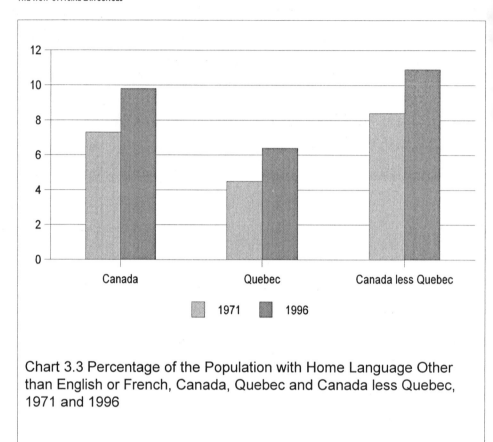

Chart 3.3 Percentage of the Population with Home Language Other than English or French, Canada, Quebec and Canada less Quebec, 1971 and 1996

Source: Appendix Table A.2.

The population that uses a non-official language most often at home (2.8 million people) is considerably smaller than the population that has a non-official language as mother tongue (4.7 million people). Many Canadians with a non-official language as mother tongue use English or French most often at home. Nevertheless, 10% of Canadians reported a non-official language as their home language in 1996, up from 7% in 1971, due to immigration. The majority of those who spoke a non-official language most often at home were living in Ontario (52%), British Columbia (17%), Quebec (16%) or Alberta (8%).

Given the ability of the three largest census metropolitan regions in Canada (Toronto, Vancouver and Montreal) to attract immigrants, it is to be expected that these regions will experience the greatest increase in the proportion of persons speaking a language other than English or French in the home. In 1996, Toronto had the highest proportion of persons speaking a non-official language in the home (25%), followed by Vancouver (22%) and Montreal (12%).

Table 3.6 Population with Home Language Other than English or French, Canada, Provinces, Territories and Canada less Quebec, 1991 and 1996

	1991		1996	
	Number ('000)	%	Number ('000)	%
Canada	2,265.1	8.4	2,784.6	9.8
Newfoundland	3.1	0.5	3.5	0.6
Prince Edward Island	0.4	0.3	0.6	0.5
Nova Scotia	10.6	1.2	13.0	1.4
New Brunswick	4.7	0.7	4.7	0.6
Quebec	396.7	5.8	452.5	6.4
Ontario	1,158.8	11.6	1,435.2	13.5
Manitoba	107.3	9.9	105.6	9.6
Saskatchewan	47.8	4.9	47.3	4.8
Alberta	193.8	7.7	218.7	8.2
British Columbia	323.0	9.9	483.3	13.1
Yukon	0.5	1.9	0.9	2.9
N.W.T.	18.4	32.0	19.4	30.3
Canada less Quebec	1,868.4	9.3	2,332.1	10.9

Source: Appendix Table A.2.

KNOWLEDGE OF NON-OFFICIAL LANGUAGES

The 1991 Census was the first to ask Canadians whether they could speak a language other than English or French. In 1996, the most common non-official languages spoken were Chinese (791,000), Italian (694,000), German (654,000) and Spanish (506,000). Many Canadians have learned a non-official language as their mother tongue. Others have acquired one or more non-official languages as second languages. Other than English or French, Spanish was the most frequently acquired second language. It was estimated that some 277,000 people could speak Spanish as a second language in 1996. German (183,000 people) and Italian (180,000 people) were the two other non-official languages most often learned as second languages. Of those who reported the ability to conduct a conversation in one or more of these three non-official languages, English or French was the mother tongue of 44% of those able to speak Spanish, 23% of those able to speak German and 23% of those able to speak Italian.

Table 3.7 The Twenty Most Common Non-official Languages, Canada, 1996

Language	Ability to Speak Number ('000)	%	Mother Tongue Number ('000)	%	Second language[1] Number ('000)	%
Chinese	791	2.8	736	2.6	55	0.2
Italian	694	2.4	514	1.8	180	0.6
German	654	2.3	471	1.6	183	0.6
Spanish	506	1.8	229	0.8	277	1.0
Portuguese	259	0.9	223	0.8	36	0.1
Polish	258	0.9	222	0.8	36	0.1
Punjabi	249	0.9	215	0.8	34	0.1
Arabic	223	0.8	166	0.6	57	0.2
Ukrainian	218	0.8	175	0.6	43	0.2
Tagalog (Pilipino)	192	0.7	158	0.6	34	0.1
Dutch	166	0.6	139	0.5	27	0.1
Greek	162	0.6	128	0.4	34	0.1
Hindi	153	0.5	48	0.2	105	0.4
Vietnamese	148	0.5	112	0.4	36	0.1
Russian	112	0.4	60	0.2	52	0.2
Cree	102	0.4	88	0.3	15	0.1
Hungarian	94	0.3	81	0.3	13	0.0
Tamil	81	0.3	72	0.3	9	0.0
Urdu	77	0.3	44	0.2	33	0.1
Persian (Farsi)	73	0.3	62	0.2	11	0.0

Sources : 1996 Census of Canada.

At the provincial level, Italian is the most commonly known non-official language in Quebec(193,000), followed by Spanish(191,000) and Arabic(92,000). Italian is also the most commonly know non-official language in Ontario(427,000), followed by Chinese(361,000) and German(250,000). These later two languages were also the most commonly spoken non-official languages in British Columbia: 277,000 spoke Chinese and 123,000 spoke German.

Knowledge of German is quite wide spread in the provinces to the East of Quebec as well as in the Prairie provinces. With the exception of Prince Edward Island and Alberta, a substantial number of speakers of Aboriginal languages are

---

1. The estimates for the second language numbers correspond to the difference between the number of people able to speak a given language and the population having that language as mother tongue.

also present—specifically, Montagnais-Naskapi in Newfoundland, Micmac in Nova Scotia and New Brunswick and Cree in Manitoba and Saskatchewan. Aboriginal languages were also wide spread in the Northwest Territories(principally Inuktitut) and the Yukon (the Athapaskan languages).

Table 3.8 Groups of the Three Most Spoken Languages Other than English or French, Canada, Provinces and Territories, 1996

		Number	%
Canada	Chinese	791,160	2.8
	Italian	694,125	2.4
	German	654,265	2.3
Newfoundland	Aboriginal languages	2,050	0.4
	German	1,250	0.2
	Spanish	865	0.2
Prince Edward Island	Dutch	590	0.4
	German	515	0.4
	Arabic	445	0.3
Nova Scotia	German	5,990	0.7
	Aboriginal languages	4,595	0.5
	Arabic	3,710	0.4
New Brunswick	Aboriginal languages	3,520	0.5
	German	3,240	0.4
	Spanish	3,215	0.4
Quebec	Italian	192,590	2.7
	Spanish	190,990	2.7
	Arabic	91,770	1.3
Ontario	Italian	427,345	4.0
	Chinese	361,370	3.4
	German	250,350	2.4
Manitoba	German	77,275	7.0
	Aboriginal languages	45,385	4.1
	Ukrainian	41,505	3.8
Saskatchewan	German	41,625	4.3
	Aboriginal languages	40,375	4.1
	Ukrainian	30,870	3.2
Alberta	German	99,165	3.7
	Chinese	83,010	3.1
	Ukrainian	49,870	1.9
British Columbia	Chinese	276,880	7.5
	German	123,100	3.3
	Punjabi	112,360	3.0
Yukon	Aboriginal languages	1,260	4.1
	German	925	3.0
	Spanish	520	1.7
Northwest Territories	Aboriginal languages	27,530	42.9
	German	560	0.9
	Spanish	355	0.6

Source: 1996 Census of Canada.

THE KNOWLEDGE OF OFFICIAL LANGUAGES

English and French, the two official languages of Canada, are the principal languages that the great majority of Canadians use to communicate. In 1996, 67% of Canada's population was able to conduct a conversation in English only, 14% in French only and 17% in both of these languages. Around 2% of people enumerated reported not knowing either of these two languages.

English-French Bilingualism

English-French bilingualism rose markedly in Canada between 1951 and 1996. The number of bilingual Canadians more than doubled during that period, rising from 1.7 million to 4.8 million, while their proportion rose from 12% to 17%.

In 1996, the rate of English-French bilingualism was highest in Quebec (38%) and New Brunswick (33%). In all other provinces and territories, bilingualism was considerably lower than the national rate of 17%.

However, the rate of bilingualism increased nearly everywhere in the country in the five-year period before the last census. Between 1991 and 1996, the proportion of the population that was bilingual grew in all provinces and territories, except Saskatchewan where it remained constant.

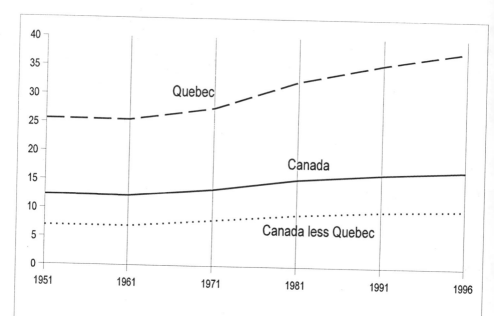

Chart 4.1 English-French Bilingualism, Canada, Quebec and Canada less Quebec, 1951-1996

Source: Appendix Table A.3.

The majority of bilingual persons live in Quebec, Ontario, British Columbia and New Brunswick. In 1996, some 90% of all bilingual persons in Canada lived in these four provinces. More than half (55%) were in Quebec, with the largest concentration in the Montreal census metropolitan area. In Ontario and New Brunswick, it is mainly in the municipalities bordering Quebec that one finds large proportions of bilingual persons. The proximity of the two official language groups is a major reason for the high rate of bilingualism in these areas. In British Columbia, more than half of bilingual persons lived in the Vancouver census metropolitan area.

Table 4.1 English-French Bilingualism, Canada, Provinces, Territories and Canada less Quebec, 1991 and 1996

	1991		1996	
	Numbers ('000)	%	Numbers ('000)	%
Canada	4,398.7	16.3	4,841.3	17.0
Newfoundland	18.5	3.3	21.3	3.9
Prince Edward Island	13.0	10.1	14.6	11.0
Nova Scotia	76.5	8.6	84.0	9.3
New Brunswick	211.5	29.5	237.8	32.6
Quebec	2,413.0	35.4	2,660.6	37.8
Ontario	1,136.2	11.4	1,234.9	11.6
Manitoba	98.8	9.2	103.1	9.4
Saskatchewan	50.8	5.2	50.8	5.2
Alberta	167.2	6.6	178.5	6.7
British Columbia	207.2	6.4	248.6	6.7
Yukon	2.6	9.3	3.2	10.5
N.W.T.	3.5	6.1	4.0	6.3
Canada less Quebec	1,985.7	9.8	2,180.7	10.2

Source: Appendix Table A.3.

The percentage of bilingual persons differs considerably from one CMA to another. Montreal has the highest rate with half of its population being bilingual. It is followed by Ottawa-Hull (44%), where there was a marked difference between the Quebec part (62%) and the Ontario part (38%). In general, the census metropolitan areas in Quebec have a higher percentage of bilingual people. Outside Quebec, Sudbury was the CMA with the highest rate of bilingualism (40%). St. John's (Newfoundland) has the lowest proportion of bilingual people (5%) of any CMA. The rate of bilingualism increased in most census metropolitan areas between 1991 and 1996.

Table 4.2 Distribution of English-French Bilingual Population, Provinces and Territories, 1996

	Number ('000)	Percentage
Canada	4,841.3	100.0
Newfoundland	21.3	0.4
Prince Edward Island	14.6	0.3
Nova Scotia	84.0	1.8
New Brunswick	237.8	4.9
Quebec	2,660.6	55.0
Ontario	1,234.9	25.5
Manitoba	103.1	2.1
Saskatchewan	50.8	1.0
Alberta	178.5	3.7
British Columbia	248.6	5.1
Yukon	3.2	0.1
Northwest Territories	4.0	0.1

Source: Calculated from Appendix Table A.3.

The rate of bilingualism for language groups varies depending on where they live: minority language groups have a higher bilingualism rate than the majority. Nationally, at 41%, the rate of bilingualism among Francophones was almost five times greater than that among Anglophones (9%). Conversely, in Quebec the English mother tongue minority has the higher rate of bilingualism. Canadians with French as a mother tongue living outside Quebec have a much higher rate of bilingualism than do those with English as a mother tongue.

The rate of bilingualism among persons with a mother tongue other than English and French remained stable in the 1991 to 1996 period. Nearly 47% of Allophones living in Quebec were bilingual, a rate almost nine times higher than that of Allophones living in the other provinces and territories.

Table 4.3 English-French Bilingualism, Census Metropolitan Areas, 1991 and 1996

Census Metropolitan Areas[1]	1991 Number ('000)	%	1996 Number ('000)	%
Calgary	52.4	7.0	59.9	7.3
Chicoutimi–Jonquière	24.0	15.1	27.6	17.4
Edmonton	64.0	7.7	63.8	7.5
Halifax	30.5	9.6	35.3	10.7
Hamilton	39.0	6.6	41.7	6.8
Kitchener	23.7	6.7	26.0	6.9
London	24.1	6.4	26.1	6.6
Montréal	1 514.4	47.7	1 634.8	49.7
Oshawa	15.7	6.6	17.8	6.7
Ottawa–Hull	398.9	42.8	440.8	44.0
Ottawa–Hull-Que.	134.7	59.8	152.4	62.1
Ottawa–Hull-Ont.	264.2	37.4	288.4	38.2
Quebec	176.4	27.7	199.3	30.0
Regina	10.6	5.6	10.7	5.6
Saint John (N.B.)	13.1	10.6	15.2	12.2
Saskatoon	13.2	6.3	14.2	6.6
Sherbrooke	50.2	36.4	56.5	39.1
St. Catharines–Niagara	28.9	8.0	30.3	8.2
St. John's (Nfld.)	7.9	4.7	9.3	5.4
Sudbury	60.0	38.5	63.7	40.1
Thunder Bay	8.3	6.8	9.3	7.4
Toronto	309.7	8.0	339.5	8.0
Trois–Rivières	29.1	21.6	33.6	24.4
Vancouver	114.2	7.2	133.5	7.4
Victoria	21.8	7.7	25.9	8.6
Windsor	27.7	10.7	29.0	10.5
Winnipeg	68.3	10.4	71.8	10.9

Sources : Census of Canada, 1991 (unpublished tabulations) and 1996.

[1]   The data for the census metropolitan areas are based on the 1996 geographic boundaries.

Table 4.4 English-French Bilingualism Among Language Groups, Canada, Quebec and Canada less Quebec, 1991 and 1996

	1991 Percentage	1996 Percentage
Canada		
Anglophones	8.5	9.0
Francophones	38.9	41.1
Allophones	11.3	11.3
Quebec		
Anglophones	59.4	62.9
Francophones	31.5	34.0
Allophones	46.6	46.8
Canada less Quebec		
Anglophones	6.4	7.0
Francophones	81.1	83.6
Allophones	5.3	5.4

Sources : Census of Canada, 1991 and 1996.

The rate of bilingualism also varies considerably by age group for Anglophones and Francophones. The difference reflects the two populations' differing ways of learning a second language. In the case of Francophones in Quebec, the rate reaches a peak at ages that correspond to high labour force participation. Thus, the rate is highest (48%) for the 20-24 age group, and stays high at subsequent ages.

For Anglophones outside Quebec, the rate of bilingualism is highest at ages corresponding to the school years. It reaches a maximum (16%) for the 15-19 age group, and declines thereafter. The lower rates in older age groups are explained, especially, by the lesser popularity or the non-existence of French immersion programmes during their school years. In the case of most recent cohorts, from kindergarten on, children could register for a French immersion programme or take French courses. Since 1971, a growing number of English schools have been providing French immersion programmes and the number of students who are registered in them has grown continuously over the years. In other words, Anglophones outside Quebec learn French as a second language mainly at school.

Table 4.5 English-French Bilingualism by Age Group Among Francophones in Quebec and Anglophones Outside Quebec, 1996

Age Group	Francophones in Quebec Percentage	Anglophones outside Quebec Percentage
Total	33.7	6.8
0 to 4	3.6	1.0
5 to 9	5.6	5.8
10 to 14	13.6	12.9
15 to 19	35.4	16.3
20 to 24	48.2	12.3
25 to 34	46.0	7.0
35 to 44	40.9	5.6
45 to 54	41.5	5.7
55 to 64	35.6	3.7
65 and plus	30.7	2.4

Source: 1996 Census of Canada, unpublished tabulations.

Outside Quebec, between 1981 and 1996, the number of elementary or secondary students enrolled in French immersion rose from 65,000 to 273,000, and the proportion rose from 2% to 7% of eligible school enrolment. Ontario accounted for more than half (55%) of all students enrolled in French immersion, while New Brunswick had the highest proportion of their students in such programmes.

Table 4.6 Enrolment in French Immersion Programmes in Public Schools, Provinces (excluding Quebec) and Territories, 1980-1981, 1990-1991 and 1995-1996

| | Eligible School Enrolment[1] | | | French Immersion Programmes | | | | | |
| | 1980–1981 | 1990–1991 | 1995–1996 | 1980–1981 | | 1990-1991 | | 1995–1996 | |
	Number	Number	Number	Number	%	Number	%	Number	%
Total[2]	3,126,091	3,646,680	3,899,657	64,761	2.1	249,523	6.8	272,660	7.0
Newfoundland	148,408	126,772	110,161	392	0.3	4,269	3.4	5,074	4.6
P.E.I.	26,296	23,835	23,757	1,280	4.9	3,371	14.1	3,385	14.2
Nova Scotia	180,384	162,232	159,882	590	0.3	5,286	3.3	10,916	6.8
N.B.	103,487	88,429	90,708	5,532	5.4	16,693	18.9	16,052	17.7
Ontario	1,739,327	1,837,082	2,001,132	46,638	2.7	133,906	7.3	151,017	7.5
Manitoba	197,894	192,122	189,805	4,286	2.2	19,604	10.2	19,020	10.0
Saskatchewan	203,652	197,857	195,994	1,603	0.8	10,713	5.4	10,404	5.3
Alberta[3]	—	481,338	513,122	4,368	—	26,924	5.6	26,676	5.2
B.C.	509,146	517,788	591,531	4,368	0.9	27,984	5.4	29,184	4.9
Yukon	4,925	5,209	6,019	35	0.7	369	7.1	452	7.5
N.W.T.	12,572	14,016	17,546	37	0.3	404	2.9	480	2.7

– Figures not available.
Source: Statistics Canada, Minority and Second Language Education, Elementary and Secondary Levels, 1995-96, unpublished tabulations.

1.   The eligible school enrolment is the total school enrolment less the number enrolled in minority language programmes. For the 1980-1981 period, the data for Alberta are excluded from the total.
2.   Excluding Quebec.
3.   In Alberta, data on French immersion programmes are available back to the 1983-1984 school year. The number of students was then 14,523 or 3.2% of the eligible school enrolment.

In the case of Francophones in Quebec, English immersion programmes are virtually non-existent. In the regular programme, English courses are mandatory from grade four of primary school. Without a doubt, job market requirements play an important role in learning English as a second language. Between 1971 and 1996, participation in the labour force increased considerably for Quebec's population, rising from 53% to 64% as a result of the increased presence of women in the labour force. This change has likely played a role in the advance of bilingualism, since nearly half of the labour force in that province is bilingual. In 1996, some 47% of the female population in the labour force in Quebec was bilingual, compared to 38% in 1971. This increase was greater than that in the male population, where the percentage of bilingual people rose from 46% to 52%.

Population Unable to Speak English or French

During the first half of the 1990s, the number of people in Canada who were unable to speak English or French has continued to increase. According to the 1996 Census, a total of 473,000 residents (2%) spoke neither official language. These included young children who could not speak any language at all, but even excluding children under five years old, there remained 386,000 people who could not speak English or French.

Table 4.7 Population Aged Five Years and Over Unable to Speak English or French, Provinces and Territories, 1996

	Number	%
Ontario	206,550	53.5
British Columbia	81,955	21.2
Quebec	53,245	13.8
Alberta	27,015	7.0
Manitoba	8,885	2.3
Saskatchewan	3,315	0.9
Northwest Territories	2,965	0.8
Nova Scotia	910	0.2
Newfoundland	445	0.1
New Brunswick	420	0.1
Yukon	50	0.0
Prince Edward Island	30	0.0
Canada	385,785	100.0

Source: 1996 Census of Canada, unpublished tabulations.

Most of the people who are unable to speak English or French live in Ontario, British Columbia, Quebec and Alberta. These provinces have been popular choices of residence for many recent immigrants: a group in which many people speak neither English nor French. Other provinces and territories have far fewer people with this language difficulty, ranging from approximately 9,000 in Manitoba to fewer than 50 each in Prince Edward Island and the Yukon.

In 1996, most of the people who were unable to speak an official language lived in large urban areas. Toronto, a city in which more than 40% of the population was born outside Canada, led the way with 164,000, followed by Vancouver (72,000) and Montreal (47,000). Edmonton and Calgary, the two major metropolitan areas in Alberta, were each home to about 12,000 people unable to speak either English or French.

In the first half of the 1990s, the number of people unable to speak English or French increased considerably in British Columbia and Ontario, and in the largest urban centres. In Toronto, for example, the number of people who spoke neither official language rose from 124,000 in 1991 to 164,000 in 1996, while in Vancouver their number was more than one and a half that of 1991. Calgary also experienced a considerable increase in this population, while smaller but significant increases were observed Montreal. Such increases have considerable implications for educational and social services (for example, language training) which are needed to integrate this population into Canadian society.

Table 4.8 Population Aged Five Years and Over Unable to Speak English or French, Canada, Provinces and Territories, 1991 and 1996

Canada, provinces and territories	1991	1996
Canada	308,535	385,785
Newfoundland	570	445
Prince Edward Island	75	30
Nova Scotia	750	910
New Brunswick	355	420
Quebec	48,225	53,245
Ontario	164,395	206,550
Manitoba	9,785	8,885
Saskatchewan	3,800	3,315
Alberta	24,475	27,015
British Columbia	52,695	81,955
Yukon	30	50
Northwest Territories	3,380	2,965

Sources : Census of Canada,1991 and 1996, unpublished tabulations.

People with Chinese, Italian or Portuguese as their mother tongues together account for more than half (55%) of all those unable to speak English or French in Canada. Chinese, the fastest-growing language group during the five years before the 1996 Census, was the mother tongue of 135,000 of these people, followed by Italian (45,000) and Portuguese (30,000).

In most of the language groups, 60% of those unable to speak an official language were women. The lower labour force participation of women is one reason for the difference in language abilities between the sexes. Men's higher labour force participation exposes them to the official languages at work and may also mean that they have better access to language training programmes in their work environment.

Languages in Canada

Table 4.9 Population Aged Five Years and Over Unable to Speak English or French, Census Metropolitan Areas, 1991 and 1996

Census Metropolitan Areas	1991	1996
Calgary	10,425	12,600
Chicoutimi–Jonquière	10	30
Edmonton	11,165	11,585
Halifax	495	660
Hamilton	7,715	7,790
Kitchener	4,885	5,075
London	3,580	3,400
Montréal	42,265	46,700
Oshawa	1,070	1,030
Ottawa–Hull	7,280	8,645
Quebec	515	770
Regina	735	710
Saint John(N.B.)	120	140
Saskatoon	910	1,00
Sherbrooke	245	275
St. Catharines–Niagara	2,185	2,500
St. John's (Newfoundland)	150	140
Sudbury	400	485
Thunder Bay	795	805
Toronto	123,845	163,560
Trois–Rivières	50	55
Vancouver	45,215	72,300
Victoria	1,495	1,940
Windsor	3,210	3,520
Winnipeg	6,800	6,335

Sources : Census of Canada,1991 and 1996, unpublished tabulations.

FACTORS AFFECTING THE EVOLUTION OF LANGUAGE GROUPS

The evolution of the size of language groups in Canada is principally the result of factors such as fertility, international migration (immigration and emigration) and also, at the provincial level, interprovincial migration. Another factor which influences the size of these groups is the parent to child transmission of the mother tongue. Since this transmission of the language is strongly influenced by whether the couple is endogamous or exogamous (based on whether both members of a couple have the same mother tongue) and by the language that is spoken most often in the home, an analysis of the evolution of the size of language groups must take into account phenomena such as exogamy and language transfers.

The most significant changes that occurred from 1951 to 1996 in the size and proportion of each language group can be summarized as follows:

English Language Group

Canada

- Considerable average annual growth during the forty-five-year period, particularly during the 1950s and 1960s (2.9% and 2.2%, respectively).

- Smaller, but substantial, average annual increases in the 1970s, 1980s and the first half of the 1990s (1.4%, 1.0% and 0.9%, respectively).

- A slight increase in the percentage of Anglophones in Canada's population, from 59% in 1951 to 60% in 1996.

Quebec

▸ Average annual growth in the Anglophone population during the first two decades of the period considered (2.5% and 1.3%, respectively).

▸ Average annual declines in the Anglophone population in both of the following decades; 1.2% during the 1970s and 1.0% during the 1980s. The average annual decline between 1991 and 1996 (slightly over 1/10 of 1%) was seven times smaller than between 1981 and 1991.

▸ Decline in the percentage of Quebec's Anglophones from 14% in 1951 to 9% in 1996.

Canada less Quebec

▸ Substantial average annual growth in the 1950s (2.9%), the 1960s (2.2%) and the 1970s (1.6%), but lower from 1981 to 1991 (1.1%) and from 1991 to 1996 (1.0%).

▸ Slight decrease in the percentage of Anglophones outside Quebec, from 78% in 1951 to 77% in 1996.

French Language Group

Canada

▸ Substantial average annual growth during the 1950s (2.6%), smaller growth during the 1960s (1.3%) and much lower growth during the two following decades (0.7% and 0.6%, respectively). During the past five-year period, growth was only 0.5%.

▸ Decline in the percentage of Francophones in Canada's population, from 29% in 1951 to 24% in 1996.

Quebec

▸ Substantial average annual increases during the 1950s (2.8%), smaller during the 1960s (1.4%).

► Much smaller average annual increases during the following twenty-five years: 0.8% from 1971 to 1981, 0.6% from 1981 to 1991 as well as over the next five-year period.

► Slight decline in the percentage of Francophones among Quebec's population, from 83% in 1951 to 82% in 1996.

Canada less Quebec

► Small average annual increases during the first two decades of the period considered (1.8% and 0.9%, respectively).

► Little change in the number of Francophones during the 1970s, an average annual increase of 0.6% during the 1980s, and a slight decrease of 0.1% during the first half of the 1990s.

► Decline in the percentage of Francophones outside Quebec, from 7% in 1951 to 4% in 1996.

Non-official Languages

Canada

► Substantial average annual increase during the 1950s (4.8%), but much smaller during the following two decades (1.4% and 1.1%, respectively).

► Remarkable increase of 1 million from 1981 to 1991 and of 623,000 from 1991 to 1996. The average annual growth was 3.2% for the 1981-1991 period and 3.0% for the 1991-1996 period.

► Increase in the percentage of Canadians with a non-official language as their mother tongue from 12% in 1951 to 17% in 1996.

Quebec

▸ Considerable average annual increase in the 1950s (9.4 %), followed by much smaller ones in the two following decades (2.8 % and 1.3 %, respectively) and a marked average annual increase of 4.2 % between 1981 and 1991 and of 2.8 % between 1991 and 1996.

▸ A rise in the proportion of Quebecers with a non-official language as their mother tongue, from 4% in 1951 to 10% in 1996.

Canada less Quebec

▸ A large average annual increase during the 1950s (4.3 %), followed by a much smaller increase in each of the next two decades (1.3 % and 1.1 %, respectively).

▸ Very large average annual increases during the next fifteen years: 3.0 % for the 1981-1991 period and 3.1 % for the 1991-1996 period.

▸ Increase in the percentage of Allophones outside Quebec from 15% in 1951 to 19% in 1996.

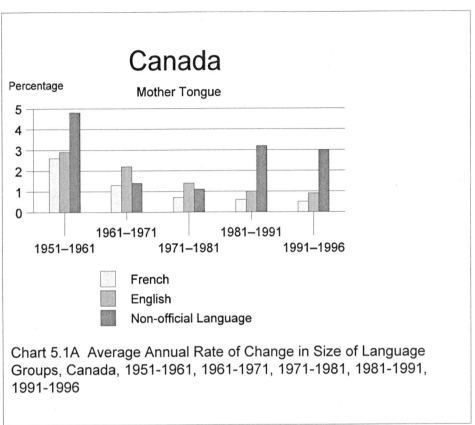

Chart 5.1A Average Annual Rate of Change in Size of Language Groups, Canada, 1951-1961, 1961-1971, 1971-1981, 1981-1991, 1991-1996

Source: Calculated from Appendix Table A.1.

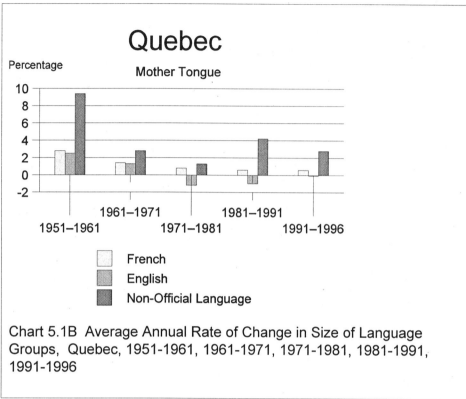

Chart 5.1B Average Annual Rate of Change in Size of Language Groups, Quebec, 1951-1961, 1961-1971, 1971-1981, 1981-1991, 1991-1996

Source: Calculated from Appendix Table A.1.

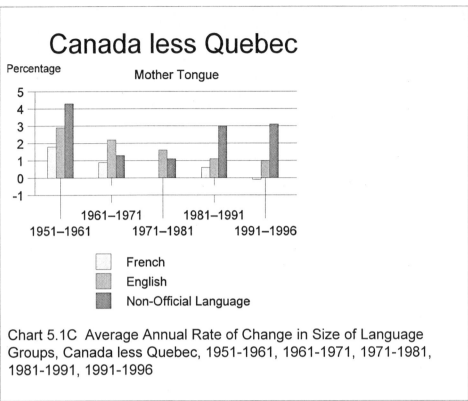

Chart 5.1C Average Annual Rate of Change in Size of Language Groups, Canada less Quebec, 1951-1961, 1961-1971, 1971-1981, 1981-1991, 1991-1996

Source: Calculated from Appendix Table A.1.

Fertility

Differences in fertility in different language groups can have the effect of favouring an increase in one group, particularly in times when there is considerable difference in the size of families. This was the case in the 1950s and early 1960s, when Francophone women tended to have more children than their Anglophone counterparts. For example, in the five years between 1956 and 1961, the total fertility rate (births per woman) was 4.3 for women whose mother tongue was French and 3.8 for those whose mother tongue was English. Reproducing at a rate that was considerably higher than that of Anglophones had the effect of maintaining the proportion of Francophones in Canada, despite an immigration pattern that favoured the English mother tongue population. This was a continuation of the higher fertility of French-Canadian women which had existed for the first half of the 20th century. The difference in fertility was largely responsible for maintaining the relative strength of the French population in Canada at about 30% between 1850 and 1950.

Table 5.1 Total Fertility Rate by Mother Tongue, Canada, Quebec and Canada less Quebec, 1956-1996

Five-year period	All Languages	Children per Woman English	French	Other
Canada				
1956–1961	3.88	3.80	4.31	3.48
1961–1966	3.51	3.48	3.66	3.40
1966–1971	2.49	2.46	2.36	2.85
1971–1976	1.98	1.95	1.85	2.32
1976–1981	1.75	1.68	1.72	2.11
1981–1986	1.66	1.67	1.49	1.94
1986–1991	1.65	1.68	1.51	1.79
1991–1996	1.69	1.67	1.64	1.85
Quebec				
1956–1961	3.99	3.26	4.22	2.79
1961–1966	3.43	3.04	3.54	2.93
1966–1971	2.26	2.09	2.27	2.58
1971–1976	1.82	1.62	1.81	2.26
1976–1981	1.71	1.46	1.71	2.04
1981–1986	1.49	1.46	1.47	1.79
1986–1991	1.51	1.54	1.49	1.78
1991–1996	1.66	1.63	1.64	1.94
Canada less Quebec				
1956–1961	3.84	3.82	4.95	3.57
1961–1966	3.55	3.50	4.34	3.46
1966–1971	2.58	2.48	2.87	2.89
1971–1976	2.04	1.96	2.12	2.33
1976–1981	1.76	1.69	1.76	2.12
1981–1986	1.72	1.68	1.60	1.96
1986–1991	1.69	1.68	1.56	1.79
1991–1996	1.70	1.68	1.57	1.84

Sources : Lachapelle, R., Evolution of Fertility Differences between Language Groups in Canada, Canadian Social Trends, No. 10, Autumn 1988, Catalogue No. 11-008E, pp. 2-8. Statistics Canada, calculations by the authors.

The fertility of French Canadian women, however, declined in the 1960s, so much so that by the end of the decade they tended to have fewer children than Anglophones. During the early 1980s, fertility among French Canadian women was nearly three times less than that of the 1950s. The historical data show a marked decrease in fertility and the convergence of fertility rates of Anglophones and Francophones in Canada. The total fertility rate for

Francophone women in the 1981-1986 period was 1.5, compared to 1.7 for Anglophone women. Whereas the data for the 1986-1991 period confirmed the lower fertility of Francophone women, those of the 1991-1996 period showed a convergence between fertility rates of the two linguistic groups. This convergence is due to the increased fertility rate of Francophone women. Demographers consider the "replacement level" fertility to correspond to a total fertility rate of 2.1. Consequently, without increases brought on by immigration or shifts from other language groups, both the Francophone and Anglophone populations in Canada would eventually decline in the long term.

The fertility of women who have a non-official language as a mother tongue has been higher than that of either Anglophones or Francophones since the mid-1960s. However, we must be careful in assessing the magnitude of the impact of this higher fertility on the growth of non-official languages in this country, since children of immigrant women who are born in Canada often learn one of the official languages as their mother tongue.

Immigration

Immigration has been the main source of the increase in the number of Canadians whose mother tongue is a non-official language. The 1996 Census showed that 65 % of those born outside Canada (excluding non-permanent residents) had a language other than English or French as their mother tongue. Immigration has also contributed significantly to the increase in the Anglophone population in Canada, but has had far less impact on the growth of the French mother tongue group. Among immigrants counted in the 1996 Census as having arrived in Canada between 1951 and 1996, there were almost nine times as many with English mother tongue (1,4 million) as with French mother tongue (159 000). In addition, all but 14% of those who immigrated to Canada during this forty-year period were living outside Quebec, in provinces and territories where the vast majority of them learn English and where many of their children have English as their mother tongue.

Immigration contributed significantly to population growth in Canada during the 1951 to 1996 period. During this period the number of immigrants in the population went from 2 million persons to nearly 5 million persons. In 1996, the immigrant proportion of the population was 17%, the highest proportion since 1951. The proportion was between 15% and 16% in each of the censuses between 1951 and 1991. While the growth in both the immigrant population (3.8%) and the population born in Canada (2.9%) was remarkable in the 1951 to 1961 period, it is between 1991 and 1996 that the different in the rate of growth of the two population was the greatest. With an average annual growth rate of 2.9% during the five year period, the growth in the population which immigrated to Canada was more than three times the rate of growth of the population born in Canada(0.8%).

Table 5.2 Size and proportion of immigrant population, Canada, 1951 to 1996

	Number ('000)	Percentage
1951	2,060	14.7
1961	2,844	15.6
1971	3,296	15.3
1981	3,867	16.1
1991	4,343	16.1
1996	4,971	17.4

Sources : Census of Canada, 1951, 1961, 1971, 1981, 1991 and 1996.

Table 5.3 Average annual growth rates of the population born in Canada and of the immigrant population, Canada, 1951 to 1996

	Born in Canada	Immigrant
1951–1961	2.9	3.8
1961–1971	1.9	1.6
1971–1981	1.1	1.7
1981–1991	1.2	1.2
1991–1996	0.8	2.9

Sources : Census of Canada, 1951, 1961, 1971, 1981, 1991 and 1996.

The knowledge of official languages is the most important factor which influences the linguistic integration into Canadian society. It's importance is, however, dependent on the period of immigration, the country of origin and the immigrants mother tongue.

In 1996, 75% of the immigrant Allophone population in Canada reported being able to conduct a conversation only in English, 4% only in French and 11% in both languages. An evaluation of the historical data regarding knowledge of official languages in the three largest census metropolitan regions (CMR) shows that, contrary to the case in Toronto and Vancouver where the percentage of the immigrant Allophone population capable of conducting a conversation in

English has hardly changed since 1971 (remaining around 80%), knowledge of official languages has evolved considerably in Montreal. In 1971, 37% of the Allophone population knew only English, 25 years later this proportion was around 22%. This situation is explained by the substantial increase in the proportion of Allophones who spoke only French (14% in 1971 compared to 25% in 1996) and who spoke both English and French (33% in 1971 and 44% in 1996). Thus while the proportion of Allophones reporting being able to conduct a conversation in English (including those reporting a knowledge of both English and French)has remained stable between 1971 (70%) and 1996 (66%), the proportion able to speak French has experienced a remarkable increase, from 48% to 69%.

Table 5.4 Immigrant Allophone population by knowledge of official languages, Montreal, Vancouver and Toronto, 1971 to 1996.

Region and year	French	English	French and English
Montreal			
1971	14.3	36.7	33.4
1981	19.5	27.6	41.8
1991	24.1	22.4	43.3
1996	24.9	21.5	44.0
Toronto			
1971	0.3	76.1	5.6
1981	0.2	80.2	5.8
1991	0.2	83.0	4.9
1996	0.1	82.4	4.6
Vancouver			
1971	0.1	84.0	5.2
1981	0.1	82.6	5.3
1991	0.1	82.6	4.3
1996	0.1	81.3	3.9

Sources: Census of Canada, 1971, 1981, 1991 and 1996.

The unique situation of Quebec is equally obvious when we look at the evolution of the knowledge of official languages among the Allophone immigrant population in the Montreal CMR. The 1996 Census shows that the longer the period that an immigrant has been in the country, the less likely they are to know only the majority official language (i.e. French) and the greater the proportion who know both official languages. While 18% of those who came to Canada between 1951 to 1960 indicated in the 1996 Census that knew only French, this portion rises to 31% among recent immigrants (those who arrived between 1991 and 1996). Similarly, the proportion of the immigrant population that indicated they knew both official languages went from 47% among those who came to Canada between 1951 and 1960 to 33% among recent immigrants. In fact, the proportion of those who spoke French was as high among recent immigrants as among those who arrived between 1951 and 1960. In the regions of Toronto and Vancouver the situation was very different. The proportion of the immigrant Allophone population who reported in the 1996 Census that they knew only the majority official language (i.e. English) was higher among those who arrived prior to the 1991 to 1996 period. The proportion who spoke both official languages was both small and diminishing. As a result, the proportion of English speakers among the immigrant Allophone population was much weaker among recent immigrants than among those who arrived between 1951 and 1960—particularly in Vancouver.

Moreover, if we focus specifically on recent Allophone immigrants to Montreal, the proportion who know French rises with each census. In the 1971 Census, 16% of recent Allophone immigrants reported knowing only French. By the 1981 Census this proportion had doubled (34%) and subsequently fluctuated around 31% in the 1991 and 1996 censuses. If we include those who know English and French, the proportion of French speakers rises from 41% in 1971 to 64% in 1996. We can observe the same trends in Toronto and Vancouver with regard to the knowledge of English among recent Allophone immigrants. However, in Vancouver, the relatively small proportion of recent Allophone immigrants with a knowledge of English in the 1971 to 1981 period is attributable, in part, to the significant rise in the proportion of immigrants of Asian origin. These immigrants, unlike subsequent Asian immigrants, were less likely to know English.

Table 5.5 Allophone immigrant population by knowledge of official languages and period of immigration reported in the 1996 Census, Montreal, Toronto and Vancouver.

Region and period of immigration	French	English	French and English
Montreal			
1951–1960	17.5	26.9	47.3
1961–1970	18.6	20.2	50.5
1971–1980	25.0	15.1	51.4
1981–1990	29.3	17.0	44.4
1991–1996	31.0	24.7	32.7
Toronto			
1951–1960	0.1	86.2	4.8
1961–1970	0.1	81.8	5.3
1971–1980	1.5	83.1	5.0
1981–1990	1.3	82.2	5.0
1991–1996	0.2	80.3	3.5
Vancouver			
1951–1960	0.1	89.8	5.6
1961–1970	0.0	86.5	5.5
1971–1980	0.1	84.4	4.1
1981–1990	0.1	79.8	4.6
1991–1996	0.7	77.0	2.4

Source: 1996 Census of Canada, unpublished tabulations.

Across the country immigration has had the effect of increasing the population with a non-official language as a mother tongue in the short run. The experience of immigrants to Canada during the early part of this century shows that in the longer term, descendants of immigrants often learn English as mother tongue. Census data show that outside Quebec, 50% of the children of Allophone women who came to the country prior to 1981, learned English as mother tongue, compared with 13% of those of Allophone women who came to Canada since 1981. However, the language transmitted to the child is above all related to the country of birth. As a result, outside Quebec, 57% of children born in Canada to Allophone immigrant women before 1981 had English as their mother tongue, compared to 16% of those born outside Canada. Among the children of women who came to Canada since 1981, 28% of those born in Canada had English as their mother tongue, compared to 5% of those born outside the country. The proportion of Allophone women whose children have

French as their mother tongue remains almost non-existent during the two periods.

In Quebec, the longer term effect of immigration is more ambiguous than for rest of the country: the children of immigrant mothers learn either English or French as mother tongue. Immigrant mothers who came to the country prior to 1981 had children who learned English as mother tongue (18%) more often than French (15%). Since that time, the situation has changed and the children of immigrant mothers learn French as mother tongue (11%) more often than English (4%).

Once again we note a significant difference according to the country of birth of the child. Among children born to immigrant women who came to Canada prior to 1981, 20% had English as their mother tongue compared to 5% of those born outside the country. These proportions where 5% and 1% respectively among the children of women who arrived since 1981. In contrast, French was transmitted as a mother tongue to a smaller proportion of children born in Canada to mothers from other countries who arrived before 1981 (17%) than to mothers who arrived since 1981 (20%). Among children born outside the country the proportions were respectively 7% and 4%.

Interprovincial Migration

Language is an important factor when considering the tendency of Canadians to move to another province. It is most vital for Quebec, since moving to that province often means settling in a more Francophone environment and leaving it often means a migration to a more Anglophone environment. The linguistic situation is significant in creating a social and cultural climate that influences the propensity of Quebecers to leave the province and that of the rest of Canadians to move to Quebec.

The 1996 Census showed that the percentage of Quebecers who had recently moved from another province was the lowest of all provinces and territories in Canada - three times less than the national average. Slightly over 1% of Quebecers were living in another province five years prior to the last census, compared with 2% in Ontario and 3% or more in the rest of the provinces and the territories.

While language is an important reason why many Francophones stay in Quebec, it can have the effect of favouring the out-migration of Anglophones from the province and facilitating the integration of the migrants in the rest of the country. In the twenty-five years prior to the 1996 Census, approximately 400,000 Anglophones left Quebec for other provinces. This number is quite high, considering that the size of the Anglophone population was 622,000 in 1996 compared to 789,000 in 1971. At the same time, Francophone departures amounted to 210,000 (5.7 million Francophones were enumerated in 1996 compared to 4.9 million in 1971).

The most significant migration of Anglophones from Quebec was during the 1976-1981 period: about 130,000 left Quebec for other provinces and only 25,000 came to Quebec from the rest of Canada, for a net loss of more than 100,000 in the Anglophone population. This migration coincided with the introduction of language legislation (Bill 101), which promoted French language status, and with favourable economic conditions in other large provinces. Between 1986 and 1996, Anglophone migration declined, resulting in net losses of 22,000 between 1986 and 1991 and of 24,000 between 1991 and 1996 - far less than in any of the three previous five-year periods.

There is relatively little movement of Quebecers with French as a mother tongue to other provinces. Much of it is compensated by the arrival of Francophones from other parts of the country. During the twenty-five years prior to the 1996 Census, Francophone departures reached a peak (about 50,000) in the 1976-1981 period. Subsequently, the number of leavers declined. Since then, the Francophone population has experienced net gains.

Table 5.6 Interprovincial Migration Between Quebec and Other Provinces and Territories by Mother Tongue, 1971-1976, 1976-1981, 1981-1986, 1986-1991 and 1991-1996

Period	Total	English	French	Other
From Quebec to others provinces	139,500	89,600	39,100	10,800
1971–76	203,000	131,500	49,900	21,600
1976–81	130,200	70,600	45,900	13,700
1981–86	107,500	53,800	37,800	16,000
1986–91	106,300	51,100	33,600	21,600
1991–96	686,500	396,600	206,300	83,700
Total				
From others provinces to Quebec				
1971–76	79,700	39,500	35,210	5,000
1976–81	61,300	25,200	31,900	4,200
1981–86	67,000	29,000	33,000	5,000
1986–91	82,000	31,600	43,000	7,400
1991–96	68,900	26,600	34,800	7,500
Total	358,900	151,900	177,910	29,100
Net migration (arrivals minus departures)				
1971–76	–59,800	–50,100	–3,890	–5,800
1976–81	–141,700	–106,300	–18,000	–17,400
1981–86	–63,200	–41,600	–12,900	–8,700
1986–91	–25,600	–22,200	5,200	–8,600
1991–96	-37,400	-24,500	1,200	-14,100
Total	-327,600	-244,700	-28,390	-54,600

Note: Population 5 years of age or more at the time of the Census.
Sources: Census of Canada, 1976, 1981, 1986, 1991 and 1996, unpublished tabulations.

If we study the destinations of Anglophones and Francophones who left Quebec in the 1991-1996 period, we find that there is very little difference in their patterns of migration. A considerable majority of both Anglophones and Francophones went to Ontario: almost two-thirds in the first case and more than a half in the second. British Columbia was the next most favoured destination for both language groups. New Brunswick, with its large French minority (a third of the population has French as mother tongue) and proximity to Quebec, was the third most favoured destination among Francophones, while Alberta was third for Anglophones leaving Quebec.

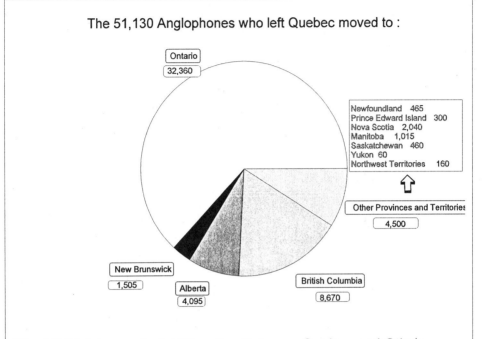

The 51,130 Anglophones who left Quebec moved to :

Ontario
32,360

Newfoundland 465
Prince Edward Island 300
Nova Scotia 2,040
Manitoba 1,015
Saskatchewan 460
Yukon 60
Northwest Territories 160

Other Provinces and Territories
4,500

New Brunswick
1,505

Alberta
4,095

British Columbia
8,670

Chart 5.2A Interprovincial Migration Between Quebec and Other Provinces and Territories by Mother Tongue, 1991-1996.

Source: 1996 Census of Canada, unpublished tabulations.

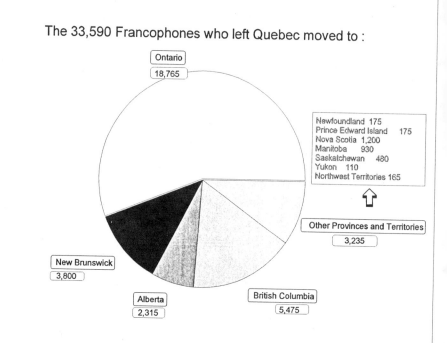

The 33,590 Francophones who left Quebec moved to :

Ontario
18,765

Newfoundland 175
Prince Edward Island 175
Nova Scotia 1,200
Manitoba 930
Saskatchewan 480
Yukon 110
Northwest Territories 165

Other Provinces and Territories
3,235

New Brunswick
3,800

Alberta
2,315

British Columbia
5,475

Chart 5.2B Interprovincial Migration Between Quebec and Other Provinces and Territories by Mother Tongue, 1991-1996

Source: 1996 Census of Canada, unpublished tabulations.

If we analyse the source of migrants coming to Quebec between 1991 and 1996, we find similar patterns of migration. The majority of Francophones (64%) and Anglophones (65%) came from Ontario.

Outside Quebec during the 1991–1996 period, Prince Edward Island, Alberta, British Columbia and the territories recorded net inflows of Francophones. The net inflow for British Columbia amounted to 6,200, substantially higher than in the previous five-year period (3,600). In Ontario, the net outflow of Francophones (6,000) was more than three times higher than the one registered during the previous five-year period (1,600). In contrast, the net outflow of Francophones from New Brunswick decelerated substantially between the two census periods, from 1,900 to 500.

Table 5.8 Interprovincial Migration of People With French as Mother Tongue, Provinces and Territories (except Quebec), 1986-1991 and 1991-1996

Provinces and territories	1986 to 1991 Migration			1991 to 1996 Migration		
	In	Out	Net	In	Out	Net
NFLD.	600	740	-140	560	890	-330
P.E.I.	555	1150	-595	730	390	340
N.S.	3,600	4,260	-660	3,400	3,750	-350
N.B.	7,780	9,650	-1,870	7,330	7,840	-510
Ontario	33,070	34,720	-1,650	24,820	30,860	-6,040
Manitoba	2,540	4,655	-2,115	2,530	3,260	-730
Sask.	1,490	2,825	-1,335	1,520	1,920	-400
Alberta	7,480	8,050	-570	6,570	6,200	370
B.C.	9,405	5,780	3,625	11,330	5,120	6,210
Yukon	300	255	-45	390	230	160
N.W.T.	575	530	-40	510	450	60

Source: 1996 Census of Canada, unpublished tabulations.

Passing on the Language

The growth and decline of language groups is affected by the tendency of one generation to pass their language on to the next. We can study this phenomenon by looking at the mother tongue of children in relation to the mother tongue of their parents. Generally, when both parents have the same official language as their mother tongue, the children almost always have that mother tongue, be it English or French. However, when parents have a non-official language as mother tongue, the children often learn one of the official languages (usually English) as mother tongue instead.

The tendency to pass on a language to children is influenced by a number of factors. Among the most important is the geographic concentration of the population which makes up a particular language group. For example, parents with a non-official language as their mother tongue are more likely to pass that language to their children if they live in a large ethnic community, than if they are isolated in a large Anglophone or Francophone population.

In Quebec, in 1996, 10% of children of less than 18 years of age were from husband-wife families in which both parents had a non-official mother tongue. About 10% of these children learned French as a mother tongue and 10% learned English. While English is transmitted as often as French, use of the latter language has expanded over the course of the last 25 years. In 1971, only 3% of children having two parents with a non-official mother tongue learned French as a mother tongue, while 14% learned English. However, Allophone parents in Quebec are more likely to transmit a non-official mother tongue to their children (76%) than those outside Quebec (65%).

In the case of the children of English-French couples, an increasing proportion are learning French as a mother tongue both in Quebec and outside this province. In Quebec, French is now transmitted more often than English as a mother tongue. In 1996, 54% of the children learned French compared to 33% who learned English. In 1971 the situation was reversed, 49% learned French and 51% learned English. Moreover, we have noted an increase in the transmission of both languages as mother tongue. In 1996, 12% of children had English and French as mother tongues compared to 10% in 1991. In the other provinces and territories, the progress of French has been even more considerable over the last 25 years. In 1971, 10% of children from English-French couples learned French as a mother tongue. In 1996 the proportion was 16%. Moreover, the proportion with both mother tongues also increased between 1991 and 1996, from 4% to 5%.

In 1996, in Quebec, children of couples in which both parents where of the Anglophone minority learned English as a mother tongue in 98% of cases, while outside Quebec those from French parents received French in 93% of cases. There have been, nonetheless, improvements in the situation of Francophones outside Quebec over the last 25 years since in 1971, 90% of children learned French as their mother tongue.

Table 5.9 Mother Tongue of Children under 18 Years of Age Living in a Husband-wife Family by Mother Tongue of Parents, Quebec, 1971, 1991 and 1996

Quebec

	Mother Tongue of Children									
	English		French		Non-official Language		French and English		Others multiples	
	Number	%	Number	%	Number	%	Number	%	Number	%
1971—Mother Tongue of Parents										
Both English	164,320	99.1	1,265	0.8	185	0.1	...	...	...	...
Both French	5,575	0.4	1,558,785	99.6	905	0.1	...	...	...	...
Both Non-official	15,425	14.1	3,120	2.9	90,545	83.0	...	...	...	...
One French, one English	34,790	50.6	33,715	49.1	225	0.3	...	...	...	...
One French, one Non-official	3,180	17.5	13,560	74.6	1,435	7.9	...	...	...	...
One English, one Non-official	11,965	93.4	195	1.5	650	5.1	...	...	...	...
1991—Mother Tongue of Parents										
Both English	63,540	98.3	725	1.1	135	0.2	240	0.4	20	0.0
Both French	1,920	0.2	1,063,545	99.7	470	0.0	575	0.1	185	0.0
Both Non-official	12,225	10.5	11,200	9.6	89,220	76.5	260	0.2	3,760	3.2
One French, one English	20,070	36.2	29,535	53.3	120	0.2	5,625	10.2	55	0.1
One French, one Non-official	2,825	9.7	21,960	75.6	2,400	8.3	735	2.5	1,115	3.8
One English, one Non-official	12,855	87.3	465	3.2	1,065	7.2	110	0.7	225	1.5
1996—Mother Tongue of Parents										
Both English	61,230	97.6	795	1.3	205	0.3	400	0.6	75	0.1
Both French	1,935	0.2	1,032,285	99.6	675	0.1	765	0.1	320	0.0
Both Non-official	12,555	9.7	12,630	9.8	98,770	76.3	575	0.4	4,990	3.9
One French, one English	19,040	33.4	30,725	53.9	50	0.1	7,130	12.5	55	0.1
One French, one Non-official	3,260	10.9	21,980	73.7	2,085	7.0	1,035	3.5	1,480	5.0
One English, one Non-official	13,510	85.0	500	3.1	1,300	8.2	165	1.0	425	2.7

Sources: Census of Canada, 1971, 1991 and 1996, unpublished tabulations.

Table 5.10 Mother Tongue of Children under 18 Years of Age Living in a Husband-wife Family by Mother Tongue of Parents, Canada less Quebec, 1971, 1991 and 1996

Canada less Quebec

	Mother Tongue of Children									
	English		French		Non-official Language		French and English		Others multiples	
	Number	%	Number	%	Number	%	Number	%	Number	%
1971—Mother Tongue of Parents										
Both English	3,299,665	99.9	1,725	0.1	2,460	0.1	...	...	...	...
Both French	27,205	9.8	249,735	90.1	185	0.1	...	...	...	...
Both Non-official	364,690	44.4	880	0.1	456,580	55.5	...	...	...	...
One French, one English	154,795	90.5	16,175	9.5	145	0.1	...	...	...	...
One French, one Non-official	25,915	76.8	5,090	15.1	2,735	8.1	...	...	...	...
One English, one Non-official	309,435	97.5	310	0.1	7,635	2.4	...	...	...	...
1991—Mother Tongue of Parents										
Both English	2,855,360	99.9	1,070	0.0	1,305	0.0	1,000	0.0	555	0.0
Both French	8,500	6.6	120,065	92.8	60	0.0	775	0.6	5	0.0
Both Non-official	238,425	34.8	540	0.1	419,125	61.2	310	0.0	26,480	3.9
One French, one English	129,635	82.4	21,075	13.4	55	0.0	6,565	4.2	0	0.0
One French, one Non-official	12,185	71.2	3,015	17.6	915	5.3	665	3.9	335	2.0
One English, one Non-official	326,100	96.0	190	0.1	9,700	2.9	175	0.1	3,510	1.0
1996—Mother Tongue of Parents										
Both English	2,905,725	99.8	1,220	0.0	1,935	0.1	1,315	0.0	975	0.0
Both French	7,220	6.5	102,360	92.8	75	0.1	550	0.5	55	0.0
Both Non-official	234,540	30.4	1,220	0.2	502,265	65.1	350	0.0	33,255	4.3
One French, one English	121,500	78.9	24,685	16.0	100	0.1	7,770	5.0	20	0.0
One French, one Non-official	11,070	68.3	3,390	20.9	760	4.7	595	3.7	390	2.4
One English, one Non-official	321,730	95.3	375	0.1	10,290	3.0	195	0.1	4,980	1.5

Sources: Census of Canada, 1971, 1991 and 1996, unpublished tabulations.

Language Shift and Exogamy

While it does not have a direct bearing on the size and growth of language groups, language shift, the tendency to speak a language at home that differs from the mother tongue, is often an indicator of future change. The language spoken most often at home will often be the one passed to the children as their mother tongue.

Language shift is an indicator of the dominance of a language and does not necessarily imply the abandonment of the mother tongue. It is therefore possible that the mother tongue is used in the home, but less often than the other.

Over the last 25 years we have seen an increase in language shift among the Francophone minority outside Quebec. In 1971, 30% of Francophones used a language other than French most often in the home, compared to 35% in 1991 and 37% in 1996. Only Francophones in British Columbia and the Yukon experienced a decline in the number of persons transferring to another language. Francophones in New Brunswick are the least likely to transfer to another language. From 1971 to 1996, the proportion having reported the use of a language other than French most often in the home has remained quite stable, going from 9% to 10%. The Anglophone minority in Quebec has also experienced an increase in language shifts over the quarter century which preceded the 1996 Census, going from 8% to 10%, however it remained relatively stable between 1991 and 1996.

In the country as a whole, the tendency of Allophones to speak either English or French most often at home declined from 1971 to 1996. In 1971, 47% of Allophones had transferred to either English or French. By 1991 this proportion had declined to 44% and declined to 40% in 1996. This decline is principally attributable to the higher rates of immigration experienced during the 1986–1996 decade. In Quebec, the situation was quite different than that of the rest of the country. A much smaller proportion of Allophones spoke a language other than their mother tongue most often in the home, 32% in 1996 and this proportion has remained constant since 1971. However, French has attracted increasing numbers of Allophones. Among those who have experienced a transfer to either English or French, a growing proportion have adopted French: 39% in 1996, compared to 37% in 1991 and 29% in 1971.

Table 5.11 Population with Home Language Different from Mother Tongue, Canada, Quebec and Canada less Quebec, 1971, 1991 and 1996

	Mother Tongue.								
	English			French			Non-official		
	1971	1991	1996	1971	1991	1996	1971	1991	1996
	%	%	%	%	%	%	%	%	%
Canada	1,2	0,7	0,7	6,2	6,2	6,2	47,2	43,8	39,7
Newfoundland	0,1	0,0	0,0	43,5	55,2	60,5	42,1	38,8	39,5
Prince Edward Island	0,3	0,1	0,1	43,2	46,8	47,6	69,8	72,1	71,0
Nova Scotia	0,3	0,1	0,1	34,1	41,7	43,4	56,6	51,1	47,6
New Brunswick	0,8	0,9	1,1	8,8	9,7	9,7	51,3	53,1	56,5
Quebec	7,5	9,9	10,2	1,6	1,2	1,1	31,9	33,1	32,3
Ontario	1,0	0,5	0,5	30,3	37,2	39,1	40,6	41,7	37,6
Manitoba	1,0	0,3	0,3	37,2	50,3	53,0	52,4	52,9	52,2
Saskatchewan	0,7	0,2	0,1	52,4	67,6	70,8	65,0	64,7	62,8
Alberta	0,6	0,2	0,3	54,1	64,8	68,0	62,2	52,0	48,3
British Columbia	0,6	0,3	0,3	73,6	73,3	72,2	60,2	47,4	39,6
Yukon	0,5	0,1	0,2	74,4	53,8	53,6	72,3	75,1	68,5
N.W.T.	1,3	0,7	0,9	53,4	54,2	60,1	20,4	21,7	25,6
Canada less Quebec	0,8	0,4	0,4	29,8	35,3	36,7	49,6	45,6	40,9

Sources: Census of Canada, 1971, 1991 and 1996, unpublished tabulations.

Among those persons living as part of a couple, the mother tongue of the partner can be the reason motivating a language shift. When both members of a couple have the same mother tongue (an endogamous couple), the language spoke most often in the home will be very commonly the mother tongue. However, when members of a couple have different mother tongues (an exogamous couple), one or the other will have to speak a different language most often in the home. Where the other spouse is also able to speak both languages it is possible the other mother tongue will also be used in the home, though less often.

In Quebec, Anglophones living in couples are much more likely than in the past to have a French mother tongue partner: 29% in 1996 compared to 15% in 1971. An increasingly smaller proportion of Anglophones in exogamous couples speak

English most often in the home: 52% in 1996 compared to 62% in 1971. Moreover, 85% of Anglophones with a Francophone partner were English-French bilinguals in 1996, compared to 75% in 1971.

Outside Quebec, Francophones living in couples have increasingly an English mother tongue partner: 36% in 1996 compared to 22% in 1971. However, in this case the frequency of language shifts has always been very high (about 96% in 1971 and 1996), as a result the increase in the number of exogamous couples will not improve the situation of French as a language spoken most often in the home. In 1996, 92% of Francophones living in exogamous couples were English-French bilinguals, while this was the case for 21% of Anglophones.

In the case of Allophones, given their increasing numbers, the phenomena of exogamy has not evolved as rapidly as in the case of Francophones and Anglophones living in a minority context. In 1996, both within and outside Quebec, more than 80% had a partner with a mother tongue other than English or French. In Quebec, more than two-thirds of Allophones in endogamous couples spoke a non-official language most often in the home, compare to 61% outside Quebec. In Quebec, 88% Allophones with an Anglophone partner spoke English most often in the home, while 65% of those with a Francophone partner had French as their home language. This situation was similar to that which existed in 1971. In 1996, among Allophones with a Francophone or Anglophone partner about three quarters where English-French bilingual. In 1971, the rate of bilingualism among Allophones in Allophone-Anglophone couples (50%) was much weaker than those in Allophone-Francophone couples (67%).

Table 5.12 A) English-French Bilingualism and Use of English as Home Language Among Anglophones Living in Couples Showing Mother Tongue of the Partner, Quebec, 1971, 1991 and 1996

Mother Tongue of the spouse [1]	Total	%	Bilingual French-English	%	English used most often in the home	%
1971						
Total	322,245	100.0	136,390	42.3	295,260	91.6
English	265,010	82.2	96,400	36.4	256,525	96.8
French	47,185	14.6	35,390	75.0	29,450	62.4
Other	10,050	3.1	4,600	45.8	9,285	92.4
1991						
Total	255,970	100.0	157,075	61.4	216,425	84.6
English	168,500	65.8	86,795	51.5	163,795	97.2
French	70,790	27.7	59,295	83.8	37,310	52.7
Other	16,680	6.5	10,985	65.9	15,320	91.8
1996						
Total	245,245	100.0	159,340	65.0	205,155	83.7
English	157,050	64.0	86,950	55.4	152,415	97.0
French	71,320	29.1	60,425	84.7	37,145	52.1
Other	16,870	6.9	11965	70.9	15,595	92.4

Sources: Census of Canada, 1971, 1991 and 1996, unpublished tabulations.

[1]   Based only on single responses to the mother tongue and home language questions.

Table 5.12 B) English-French Bilingualism and Use of French as Home Language Among Francophones Living in Couples Showing Mother Tongue of the Partner, Canada less Quebec, 1971, 1991 and 1996

Mother Tongue of the Spouse [1]	Francophones Living in Couples					
	Total	%	Bilingual French–English	%	French used most often in the Home	%
1971						
Total	398,940	100.0	349,100	87.5	255,840	64.1
English	86,580	21.7	89,420	103.3	8,370	9.7
French	292,320	73.3	239,985	82.1	245,455	84.0
Other	20,040	5.0	19,695	98.3	2,015	10.1
1991						
Total	511,510	100.0	441,345	86.3	281,375	55.0
English	177,800	35.0	162,260	91.3	15,425	8.7
French	311,940	61.4	259,875	83.3	263,620	84.5
Other	21,770	4.3	19,210	88.2	2,330	10.7
1996						
Total	507,660	100.0	447,955	88.2	274,310	54.0
English	184,610	36.4	169,790	92.0	17,465	9.5
French	300,690	59.2	258,040	85.8	254,125	84.5
Other	22,360	4.4	20,125	90.0	2,720	12.2

Sources: Census of Canada, 1971, 1991 and 1996, unpublished tabulations.

---

[1]   Based only on single responses to the mother tongue and home language questions.

Table 5.12 C) English-French Bilingualism and Use of English, French or a Non-official Language as Home Language Among Allophones Living in Couple Showing Mother Tongue of the Partner, Quebec, 1971, 1991 and 1996

					Allophones Living in Couples					
					Language used most often in the home					
Mother Tongue of the Spouse [1]	Total	%	Bilingual French-English	%	French Number	%	English Number	%	Non-official Number	%
1971										
Total	189,890	100.0	61,915	32.6	17,510	9.2	43,685	23.0	128,690	67.8
English	9,980	5.3	4,970	49.8	265	2.7	8,800	88.2	910	9.1
French	13,935	7.3	9,325	66.9	8,585	61.6	4,170	29.9	1,180	8.5
Other	165,975	87.4	47,620	28.7	8,660	5.2	30,715	18.5	126,600	76.3
1991										
Total	294,350	100.0	135,825	46.1	37,295	12.7	64,910	22.1	170,435	57.9
English	16,680	5.7	11,770	70.6	580	3.5	14,580	87.4	670	4.0
French	32,525	11.0	23,870	73.4	21,035	64.7	6,870	21.1	2,260	6.9
Other	245,145	83.3	100,185	40.9	15,680	6.4	43,460	17.7	167,505	68.3
1996										
Total	326,360	100.0	154,425	47.3	40,280	12.3	69,035	21.2	191,230	58.6
English	16,870	5.2	12,390	73.4	655	3.9	14,875	88.2	810	4.8
French	33,875	10.4	25,995	76.7	21,905	64.7	7,430	21.9	1,640	4.8
Other	275,615	84.5	116,040	42.1	17,720	6.4	46,730	17.0	188,780	68.5

Source: Census of Canada, 1971, 1991 and 1996, unpublished tabulations.

---

1. Based only on single responses to the mother tongue and home language questions.

Table 5.12 D) English-French Bilingualism and Use of English, French or a Non-official Language as Home Language Among Allophones Living in Couple Showing Mother Tongue of the Partner, Canada less Quebec, 1971, 1991 and 1996

Allophones Living in Couples

Mother Tongue of Spouse[1]	Total Number	%	Bilingual English-French Number	%	Language Spoken Most Often in the Home					
					French Number	%	English Number	%	Non-official Number	%
1971										
Total	1,365,740	100.0	48,045	3.5	2,885	0.2	707,875	51.8	654,985	48.0
English	211,740	15.5	10,830	5.1	135	0.1	204,310	96.5	7,305	3.4
French	19,630	1.4	3,720	19.0	1,140	5.8	17,515	89.2	975	5.0
Other	1,134,370	83.1	33,495	3.0	1,610	0.1	486,050	42.8	646,705	57.0
1991										
Total	1,945,755	100.0	85,835	29.2	2,525	0.1	949,240	48.8	881,150	45.3
English	373,390	19.2	28,120	168.6	145	0.0	357,340	95.7	10,370	2.8
French	21,760	1.1	5,600	25.7	1,345	6.2	18,635	85.6	995	4.6
Other	1,550,605	79.7	52,115	3.4	1,035	0.1	573,265	37.0	869,785	56.1
1996										
Total	2,199,345	100.0	96,790	4.4	2,935	0.1	956,385	43.5	1,105,795	50.3
English	384,010	17.5	31,085	8.1	155	0.0	369,760	96.3	8,005	2.1
French	22,360	1.0	6,210	27.8	1,505	6.7	19,290	86.3	785	3.5
Other	1,792,975	81.5	59,495	3.3	1,275	0.1	567,335	31.6	1,097,005	61.2

Source: Census of Canada, 1971, 1991 and 1996, unpublished tabulations.

1. Based only on single responses to the mother tongue and home language questions.

Overview of factors

Despite an increasing number of Francophones in Canada, their relative share of the Canadian population declined between 1951 and 1996. The two main factors that contributed to this decline were the reduction in the fertility of Francophone women and the immigration to Canada of many people whose mother tongue is a language other than French. The arrival of these immigrants added considerably to the Anglophone population, and to the population with a non-official language as mother tongue, but augmented the Francophone population only slightly.

In Quebec, the number of Francophones increased considerably, but the percentage has fluctuated between 80% and 83% in the 1951 to 1996 period. The departure of many Anglophones has enabled the Francophone population to maintain its relative strength despite a decrease in the fertility of Francophone women, and an increase in the Allophone population, particularly in the last fifteen years.

Outside Quebec, the number of Francophones has grown, but the percentage has declined steadily. This decline which, until 1991, resulted mainly from increases in the non-Francophone population which gained considerable numbers through immigration, is now also explained by a decrease in the numbers of Francophones. Besides the decrease of the fertility of Francophone women, the high tendency of children born to English-French couples to learn English as their mother tongue has contributed to this decline.

The size of the Anglophone population in Canada increased considerably between 1951 and 1996, while the percentage (60% in 1996) changed very little. Immigration and the tendency of children of immigrants to learn English as mother tongue contributed substantially to the increase in Anglophones. In Quebec, the English mother tongue group has declined both in number and percentage due to strong migration to other provinces and territories.

The population with a non-official language as mother tongue increased both in number and in proportion among the Canadian population. Immigration is the main source of growth for most language groups other than English or French, the majority of immigrants having a non-official language as mother tongue.

CONCLUSION

The last forty-five years, from 1951 to 1996, were a time of considerable change in the linguistic portrait of our country. During this period the Canadian population more than doubled, from fourteen to twenty-nine million people. Such increases rarely occur without an effect on the composition of the population. This study has presented an overview of important changes, as well as a portrait of the current language situation.

The factors which have led to the present situation of English, French and other language groups—fertility, migration (international and interprovincial) and the transmission of a language to the next generation—will continue to play a vital role in the future evolution of language groups all over the country. It is difficult to imagine a reasonable scenario which would reverse the trend towards a reduction in the proportion of Francophones in the overall population of the country.

The fluctuations in the percentage of Allophones in the Canadian population are due to immigration. In the short run, immigration increases this population, but in the long run the children and grandchildren of immigrants tend to learn one of the official languages as mother tongue. Thus, heavy immigration could maintain or increase the percentage of Canadian Allophones briefly, but if the patterns observed for immigrants continue, a decline in their percentage will eventually take place.

The population whose mother tongue is English has grown as a result of immigration, as people with English mother tongue move to Canada, and as the descendants of immigrants from other language groups move toward using the language of the North American majority. While the short-term impact of heavy immigration is to increase the non-official language groups, use of the English language has experienced considerable long-term growth through immigration.

If immigration continues to favour the growth of the Anglophone group and fertility of the two official language groups remains similar to current levels, it is likely that both the number and proportion of Anglophones will increase in the future.

GLOSSARY

Mother Tongue	First language learned at home in childhood and still understood by the individual at the time of the census.
Home Language	Language spoken most often at home by the individual at the time of the census.
Knowledge of Official Languages	Refers to the ability to conduct a conversation in English only, in French only, in both English and French or in neither of the official languages of Canada.
Knowledge of Non-official Languages	Refers to all languages, other than English or French, in which the respondent can conduct a conversation.
First Official Language Spoken	Refers to the official language actually spoken which, in most cases, was first learned by the individual.
Anglophone	Person with English as mother tongue.
Francophone	Person with French as mother tongue.
Allophone	Person with a non-official language as mother tongue.

English Speaker	Person who is able to conduct a conversation in English.
French Speaker	Person who is able to conduct a conversation in French.
Language Group	Population with a common mother tongue.
Language Transfer	Refers to the use of a language most often at home which is different from the mother tongue.
Exogamy	Situation occurring when partners in a couple have different mother tongues.

DATA QUALITY

Statistics used for this study come from the sample data from the 1971 to 1996 Censuses. For the 1971 Census, they are taken from responses obtained from one third of Canadian households that completed the long form questionnaire and, since the 1981 Census, from one fifth. The mother tongue data from this sample, especially for the 1991 and 1996 Censuses, are considered to be more accurate than those collected from the entire population, since there are far fewer multiple responses. Evaluations have shown that the number of people with more than one mother tongue is overestimated for households completing the short form questionnaire. The difference in the proportion of multiple responses obtained from each source is probably due to the fact that, in the short form, the question on mother tongue was the only language question asked while on the long form, other language questions were asked before the question on mother tongue. Respondents would be less likely to indicate two or more mother tongues if they were first able to indicate their language knowledge. However, the direction of most trends is consistent regardless of the data base used.

Since the 1981 Census, data from the 20% sample data base exclude institutional residents. Consequently, the figures for this census and the following ones are lower than they would be with this population included, and are not strictly comparable with previous censuses.

In the trend analysis, multiple responses were evenly divided between the languages reported. For example, if a given number of respondents provided English and French as their mother tongue or home language, half were assigned to the English category and half to the French. The same procedure was followed for multiple responses which included an official language and a non-official language.

The 1991 Census included, for the first time, residents of Canada who were non-permanent residents. These include people who hold student or employment authorizations, Minister's permits or who are refugee claimants, as well as their dependants. Prior to 1991, such people were considered foreign residents and were not enumerated. Since many of these people have non-official languages as mother tongue, their inclusion boosts the percentage of this population slightly for 1991 and 1996.

APPENDIX OF TABLES

Table A.1
Population by Mother Tongue, Canada, Provinces, Territories and Canada less Quebec, 1951 to 1996

	Total	French		English		Non-official Language	
		Number	%	Number	%	Number	%
Canada							
1951	14,009,429	4,068,850	29.0	8,280,809	59.1	1,659,770	11.8
1961	18,238,247	5,123,151	28.1	10,660,534	58.5	2,454,562	13.5
1971	21,568,310	5,792,710	26.9	12,967,445	60.1	2,808,155	13.0
1981	24,083,505	6,177,795	25.7	14,784,810	61.4	3,120,900	13.0
1991	26,994,040	6,562,065	24.3	16,311,210	60.4	4,120,770	15.3
1996	28,528,130	6,711,644	23.5	17,072,432	59.8	4,744,059	16.6
Newfoundland							
1951	361,416	2,321	0.6	357,328	98.9	1,767	0.5
1961	457,853	3,150	0.7	451,530	98.6	3,173	0.7
1971	522,105	3,610	0.7	514,415	98.5	4,080	0.8
1981	563,745	2,580	0.5	557,040	98.8	4,125	0.7
1991	563,925	2,855	0.5	555,925	98.6	5,140	0.9
1996	547,160	2,440	0.4	539,048	98.5	5,663	1.0
Prince Edward Island							
1951	98,429	8,477	8.6	89,241	90.7	711	0.7
1961	104,629	7,958	7.6	95,564	91.3	1,107	1.1
1971	111,640	7,360	6.6	103,115	92.4	1,165	1.1
1981	121,220	5,835	4.8	114,095	94.1	1,295	1.1
1991	128,100	5,750	4.5	120,770	94.3	1,585	1.2
1996	132,860	5,722	4.3	125,017	94.1	2,137	1.6

Table A.1
Population by Mother Tongue, Canada, Provinces, Territories and Canada less Quebec, 1951 to 1996

| | Total | | Mother Tongue | | | | | |
| | | | French | | English | | Non-official language | |
			Number	%	Number	%	Number	%
Nova Scotia								
1951	642,584		38,945	6.1	588,610	91.6	15,029	2.3
1961	737,007		39,568	5.4	680,233	92.3	17,206	2.3
1971	788,960		39,585	5.0	733,195	93.0	16,180	2.1
1981	839,800		35,385	4.2	786,725	93.7	17,695	2.1
1991	890,945		37,525	4.2	831,575	93.3	21,845	2.5
1996	899,970		36,311	4.0	838,283	93.1	25,376	2.8
New Brunswick								
1951	515,697		185,110	35.9	325,412	63.1	5,175	1.0
1961	597,936		210,530	35.2	378,633	63.3	8,773	1.5
1971	634,560		214,720	33.8	411,275	64.8	8,565	1.3
1981	689,370		231,970	33.6	448,885	65.1	8,515	1.2
1991	716,500		243,690	34.0	462,875	64.6	9,935	1.4
1996	729,630		242,408	33.2	476,396	65.3	10,826	1.5
Quebec								
1951	4,055,681		3,347,030	82.5	558,256	13.8	150,395	3.7
1961	5,259,211		4,269,689	81.2	697,402	13.3	292,120	5.6
1971	6,027,765		4,866,410	80.7	788,830	13.1	372,525	6.2
1981	6,369,055		5,254,195	82.5	693,600	10.9	421,265	6.6
1991	6,810,305		5,585,650	82.0	626,200	9.2	598,455	8.8
1996	7,045,085		5,741,438	81.5	621,858	8.8	681,790	9.7

Table A.1
Population by Mother Tongue, Canada, Provinces, Territories and Canada less Quebec, 1951 to 1996

	Total	French		English		Non-official language	
		Number	%	Number	%	Number	%
Ontario							
1951	4,597,542	341,502	7.4	3,755,442	81.7	500,598	10.9
1961	6,236,092	425,302	6.8	4,834,623	77.5	976,167	15.7
1971	7,703,110	482,350	6.3	5,967,725	77.5	1,253,035	16.3
1981	8,534,260	465,335	5.5	6,611,990	77.5	1,456,940	17.1
1991	9,977,055	503,345	5.0	7,443,540	74.6	2,030,170	20.3
1996	10,642,790	499,689	4.7	7,777,734	73.1	2,365,367	22.2
Manitoba							
1951	776,541	54,199	7.0	467,892	60.3	254,450	32.8
1961	921,686	60,899	6.6	584,526	63.4	276,260	30.0
1971	988,245	60,485	6.1	662,130	67.0	265,630	26.8
1981	1,013,700	51,620	5.1	731,500	72.2	230,575	22.7
1991	1,079,390	50,775	4.7	793,325	73.5	235,285	21.8
1996	1,100,295	49,100	4.5	822,258	74.7	228,940	20.8
Saskatchewan							
1951	831,728	36,815	4.4	515,873	62.0	279,040	33.5
1961	925,181	36,163	3.9	638,156	69.0	250,862	27.1
1971	926,245	31,795	3.4	685,025	74.0	209,425	22.6
1981	956,445	25,090	2.6	767,110	80.2	164,250	17.2
1991	976,040	21,795	2.2	812,600	83.3	141,645	14.5
1996	976,615	19,901	2.0	823,746	84.3	132,968	13.6

Table A.1

Population by Mother Tongue, Canada, Provinces, Territories and Canada less Quebec, 1951 to 1996

	Total	French		English		Non-official language	
		Mother Tongue					
		Number	%	Number	%	Number	%
Alberta							
1951	939,501	34,196	3.6	648,413	69.0	256,892	27.3
1961	1,331,944	42,276	3.2	962,319	72.2	327,349	24.6
1971	1,627,875	46,750	2.9	1,262,840	77.6	318,285	19.5
1981	2,213,640	60,605	2.7	1,800,870	81.4	352,165	15.9
1991	2,519,185	56,730	2.3	2,045,905	81.2	416,550	16.5
1996	2,669,195	55,290	2.0	2,175,758	81.5	438,148	16.4
British Columbia							
1951	1,165,210	19,366	1.7	963,920	82.7	181,924	15.6
1961	1,629 082	26,179	1.6	1,318 498	80.9	284,405	17.5
1971	2,184,625	38,035	1.7	1,807,240	82.7	339,350	15.5
1981	2,713,620	43,415	1.6	2,228,185	82.1	442,025	16.3
1991	3,247,495	51,585	1.6	2,562,240	78.9	633,665	19.5
1996	3,689,755	56,755	1.5	2,809,398	76.1	823,603	22.3
Yukon							
1951	9,096	308	3.4	6,618	72.8	2,170	23.9
1961	14,628	443	3.0	10,869	74.3	3,316	22.7
1971	18,390	450	2.4	15,340	83.4	2,600	14.1
1981	23,080	530	2.3	20,185	87.5	2,365	10.2
1991	27,665	905	3.3	24,550	88.7	2,210	8.0
1996	30,650	1,170	3.8	26,613	86.8	2,868	9.4

Table A.1

Population by Mother Tongue, Canada, Provinces, Territories and Canada less Quebec, 1951 to 1996

| | Total | | Mother Tongue | | | | | | |
| | | | French | | English | | Non-official language | | |
	Number	%	Number	%	Number	%	Number	%
Northwest Territories								
1951	16,004		581	3.6	3,804	23.8	11,619	72.6
1961	22,998		994	4.3	8,181	35.6	13,823	60.1
1971	34,805		1,160	3.3	16,305	46.8	17,340	49.8
1981	45,535		1,225	2.7	24,635	54.1	19,675	43.2
1991	57,435		1,455	2.5	31,705	55.2	24,280	42.3
1996	64,125		1,421	2.2	36,326	56.6	26,378	41.1
Canada less Quebec								
1951	9,953,748		721,820	7.3	7,722,553	77.6	1,509,375	15.2
1961	12,979,036		853,462	6.6	9,963,132	76.8	2,162,442	16.7
1971	15,540,545		926,400	6.0	12,184,625	78.4	2,429,520	15.7
1981	17,714,450		923,605	5.2	14,091,215	79.5	2,699,635	15.2
1991	20,183,735		976,415	4.8	15,685,005	77.7	3,522,315	17.5
1996	21,483,045		970,207	4.5	16,450,574	76.6	4,062,269	18.9

Note: Since the 1981 Census, the figures exclude institutional residents, which represent approximately 1% of the population.

Sources: Census of Canada, 1951, 1961, 1971, 1981, 1991 and 1996.

Table A.2

Population by Home Language, Canada, Provinces, Territories and Canada less Quebec, 1971 to 1996

	Total	French		English		Non-official language	
		Number	%	Number	%	Number	%
Canada							
1971	21,568,310	5,546,025	25.7	14,446,235	67.0	1,576,050	7.3
1981	24,083,495	5,919,855	24.6	16,375,315	68.0	1,788,325	7.4
1991	26,994,045	6,288,430	23.3	18,440,540	68.3	2,265,075	8.4
1996	28,528,120	6,448,603	22.6	19,294,873	67.6	2,784,643	9.8
Newfoundland							
1971	522,100	2,295	0.4	517,210	99.1	2,595	0.5
1981	563,750	1,845	0.3	559,390	99.2	2,515	0.4
1991	563,935	1,340	0.2	559,505	99.2	3,095	0.5
1996	547,155	1,018	0.1	542,628	99.2	3,510	0.6
Prince Edward Island							
1971	111,640	4,405	3.9	106,795	95.7	440	0.4
1981	121,230	3,745	3.1	117,040	96.5	450	0.4
1991	128,105	3,050	2.4	124,620	97.3	440	0.3
1996	132,855	3,045	2.3	129,190	97.2	620	0.5
Nova Scotia							
1971	788,960	27,220	3.5	753,725	95.5	8,015	1.0
1981	839,800	24,435	2.9	806,490	96.0	8,875	1.1
1991	890,945	22,260	2.5	858,130	96.3	10,555	1.2
1996	899,970	20,710	2.3	866,260	96.3	13,000	1.4

Home Language

Table A.3
Population by Knowledge of Official Languages, Canada, Provinces, Territories and Canada less Quebec, 1951 to 1996

	Total	French Only		Knowledge of Official Languages English Only		French and English		Neither French, nor English	
	Number	Number	%	Number	%	Number	%	Number	%
Canada									
1951	14,009,429	2,741,812	19.6	9,387,395	67.0	1,727,447	12.3	152,775	1.1
1961	18,238,247	3,489,866	19.1	12,284,762	67.4	2,231,172	12.2	232,447	1.3
1971	21,568,310	3,879,255	18.0	14,469,540	67.1	2,900,155	13.4	319,360	1.5
1981	24,083,495	3,987,245	16.6	16,122,895	66.9	3,681,960	15.3	291,395	1.2
1991	26,994,035	4,110,300	15.2	18,106,760	67.1	4,398,655	16.3	378,320	1.4
1996	28,528,100	4,079,080	14.3	19,134,245	67.1	4,841,310	17.0	473,465	1.7
Newfoundland									
1951	361,416	153	0.0	356,377	98.6	3,990	1.1	896	0.2
1961	457,853	522	0.1	450,945	98.5	5,299	1.2	1,087	0.2
1971	522,105	510	0.1	511,620	98.0	9,350	1.8	625	0.1
1981	563,750	145	0.0	550,335	97.6	12,840	2.3	430	0.1
1991	563,940	240	0.0	544,425	96.5	18,495	3.3	780	0.1
1996	547,155	155	0.0	525,190	96.0	21,260	3.9	550	0.1
Prince Edward Island									
1951	98,429	914	0.9	88,743	90.2	8,745	8.9	27	0.0
1961	104,629	1,219	1.2	95,296	91.1	7,938	7.6	176	0.2
1971	111,640	680	0.6	101,820	91.2	9,110	8.2	30	0.0
1981	121,225	205	0.2	111,200	91.7	9,780	8.1	40	0.0
1991	128,095	270	0.2	114,795	89.6	12,950	10.1	80	0.1
1996	132,855	170	0.1	118,080	88.9	14,570	11.0	35	0.0

Table A.2

Population by Home Language, Canada, Provinces, Territories and Canada less Quebec, 1951 to 1996

	Total		Home Language					
		French		English		Non-official language	
		Number	%	Number	%	Number	%
Northwest Territories							
1971	34,800	585	1.7	20,225	58.1	13,990	40.2
1981	45,535	630	1.4	28,670	63.0	16,235	35.7
1991	57,435	680	1.2	38,355	66.8	18,400	32.0
1996	64,120	607	0.9	44,112	68.8	19,402	30.3
Canada less Quebec							
1971	15,540,545	675,925	4.3	13,558,360	87.2	1,306,260	8.4
1981	17,714,420	666,785	3.8	15,568,530	87.9	1,479,105	8.3
1991	20,183,745	636,640	3.2	17,678,730	87.6	1,868,380	9.3
1996	21,483,035	618,522	2.9	18,532,417	86.3	2,332,097	10.9

Note: Since the 1981 Census, the figures exclude institutional residents, which represent approximately 1% of the population.
Sources: Census of Canada, 1971, 1981, 1991 and 1996.

Table A.2

Population by Home Language, Canada, Provinces, Territories and Canada less Quebec, 1971 to 1996

	Total		French		English		Non-official language	
	Number	%	Number	%	Number	%	Number	%
Saskatchewan								
1971	926,240		15,930	1.7	832,515	89.9	77,795	8.4
1981	956,435		10,295	1.1	884,760	92.5	61,380	6.4
1991	976,030		7,155	0.7	921,085	94.4	47,790	4.9
1996	976,615		5,828	0.6	923,443	94.6	47,343	4.8
Alberta								
1971	1,627,870		22,700	1.4	1,477,960	90.8	127,210	7.8
1981	2,213,645		29,690	1.3	2,024,090	91.4	159,860	7.2
1991	2,519,180		20,180	0.8	2,305,200	91.5	193,800	7.7
1996	2,669,195		17,822	0.6	2,432,682	91.1	218,692	8.2
British Columbia								
1971	2,184,620		11,505	0.5	2,027,120	92.8	145,995	6.7
1981	2,713,620		15,090	0.6	2,479,555	91.4	218,980	8.1
1991	3,247,495		14,555	0.4	2,909,930	89.6	323,010	9.9
1996	3,689,760		16,586	0.4	3,189,883	86.5	483,291	13.1
Yukon								
1971	18,395		135	0.7	17,470	95.0	790	4.3
1981	23,075		240	1.0	22,075	95.7	760	3.3
1991	27,645		390	1.4	26,735	96.7	520	1.9
1996	30,655		543	1.8	29,240	95.4	873	2.9

Table A.2
Population by Home Language, Canada, Provinces, Territories and Canada less Quebec, 1971 to 1996

	Total	French		English		Non-official language	
	Number	Number	%	Number	%	Number	%
New Brunswick							
1971	634,560	199,080	31.4	430,720	67.9	4,760	0.8
1981	689,380	216,745	31.4	468,105	67.9	4,530	0.7
1991	716,490	223,265	31.2	488,570	68.2	4,660	0.7
1996	729,625	222,441	30.1	502,526	68.9	4,658	0.6
Quebec							
1971	6,027,765	4,870,100	80.8	887,875	14.7	269,790	4.5
1981	6,369,075	5,253,070	82.5	806,785	12.7	309,220	4.9
1991	6,810,300	5,651,795	83.0	761,815	11.2	396,695	5.8
1996	7,045,085	5,830,082	82.8	762,457	10.8	452,547	6.4
Ontario							
1971	7,703,105	352,465	4.6	6,558,060	85.1	792,580	10.3
1981	8,534,270	333,050	3.9	7,310,060	85.7	891,160	10.4
1991	9,977,055	318,705	3.2	8,499,515	85.2	1,158,830	11.6
1996	10,642,790	306,790	2.9	8,900,845	83.6	1,435,155	13.5
Manitoba							
1971	988,245	39,600	4.0	816,560	82.6	132,085	13.4
1981	1,013,705	31,030	3.1	868,295	85.7	114,380	11.3
1991	1,079,395	25,045	2.3	947,090	87.7	107,265	9.9
1996	1,100,295	23,133	2.1	971,608	88.3	105,553	9.6

Table A.3
Population by Knowledge of Official Languages, Canada, Provinces, Territories and Canada less Quebec, 1951 to 1996

| | Total | Knowledge of Official Languages | | | | | | | |
| | | French Only | | English Only | | French and English | | Neither French, nor English | |
		Number	%	Number	%	Number	%	Number	%
Nova Scotia									
1951	642,584	7,462	1.2	595,257	92.6	39,524	6.2	341	0.0
1961	737,007	5,938	0.8	684,805	92.9	44,987	6.1	1,277	0.2
1971	788,955	4,185	0.5	730,700	92.6	53,035	6.7	1,035	0.1
1981	839,795	1,880	0.2	774,760	92.3	62,350	7.4	805	0.1
1991	890,945	1,580	0.2	811,870	91.1	76,465	8.6	1,030	0.1
1996	899,970	1,375	0.2	813,320	90.4	83,980	9.3	1,295	0.1
New Brunswick									
1951	515,697	100,712	19.5	318,560	61.8	96,095	18.6	330	0.1
1961	597,936	112,054	18.7	370,922	62.0	113,495	19.0	1,465	0.2
1971	634,555	100,985	15.9	396,855	62.5	136,115	21.5	600	0.1
1981	689,370	89,340	13.0	417,025	60.5	182,550	26.5	455	0.1
1991	716,495	89,500	12.5	414,955	57.9	211,525	29.5	515	0.1
1996	729,625	73,410	10.1	417,970	57.3	237,765	32.6	480	0.1
Quebec									
1951	4,055,681	2,534,242	62.5	462,813	11.4	1,038,130	25.6	20,496	0.5
1961	5,259,211	3,254,850	61.9	608,635	11.6	1,338,878	25.5	56,848	1.1
1971	6,027,765	3,668,015	60.9	632,515	10.5	1,663,790	27.6	63,445	1.1
1981	6,369,065	3,826,605	60.1	426,240	6.7	2,065,105	32.4	51,115	0.8
1991	6,810,300	3,958,930	58.1	373,755	5.5	2,412,985	35.4	64,630	0.9
1996	7,045,075	3,951,710	56.1	358,505	5.1	2,660,590	37.8	74,270	1.1

Table A.3

Population by Knowledge of Official Languages, Canada, Provinces, Territories and Canada less Quebec, 1951 to 1996

	Total	Knowledge of Official Languages							
		French Only		English Only		French and English		Neither French, nor English	
		Number	%	Number	%	Number	%	Number	%
Ontario									
1951	4,597,542	78,974	1.7	4,115,584	89.5	359,965	7.8	43,019	0.9
1961	6,236,092	95,236	1.5	5,548,766	89.0	493,270	7.9	98,820	1.6
1971	7,703,100	92,845	1.2	6,724,100	87.3	716,065	9.3	170,090	2.2
1981	8,534,265	60,535	0.7	7,401,070	86.7	924,475	10.8	148,185	1.7
1991	9,977,055	54,245	0.5	8,593,635	86.1	1,136,245	11.4	192,930	1.9
1996	10,642,785	46,940	0.4	9,116,165	85.7	1,234,895	11.6	244,785	2.3
Manitoba									
1951	776,541	7,869	1.0	685,914	88.3	58,441	7.5	24,317	3.1
1961	921,686	7,954	0.9	825,955	89.6	68,368	7.4	19,409	2.1
1971	988,255	5,020	0.5	881,715	89.2	80,935	8.2	20,585	2.1
1981	1,013,710	2,620	0.3	915,760	90.3	79,990	7.9	15,340	1.5
1991	1,079,390	1,905	0.2	965,100	89.4	98,800	9.2	13,585	1.3
1996	1,100,295	1,495	0.1	983,820	89.4	103,140	9.4	11,840	1.1
Saskatchewan									
1951	831,728	4,656	0.6	767,248	92.2	40,789	4.9	19,035	2.3
1961	925,181	3,853	0.4	865,821	93.6	42,074	4.5	13,433	1.5
1971	926,235	1,825	0.2	867,315	93.6	45,985	5.0	11,110	1.2
1981	956,435	705	0.1	904,900	94.6	43,650	4.6	7,180	0.8
1991	976,035	450	0.0	919,070	94.2	50,800	5.2	5,715	0.6
1996	976,615	345	0.0	920,555	94.3	50,770	5.2	4,945	0.5

Table A.3

Population by Knowledge of Official Languages, Canada, Provinces, Territories and Canada less Quebec, 1951 to 1996

	Total	French Only		English Only		French and English		Neither French, nor English	
	Number	Number	%	Number	%	Number	%	Number	%
Alberta									
1951	939,501	5,922	0.6	868,696	92.5	40,785	4.3	24,098	2.6
1961	1,331,944	5,534	0.4	1,253,824	94.1	56,920	4.3	15,666	1.2
1971	1,627,875	3,310	0.2	1,525,575	93.7	81,000	5.0	17,990	1.1
1981	2,213,650	3,700	0.2	2,045,060	92.4	142,465	6.4	22,425	1.0
1991	2,519,180	1,940	0.1	2,318,935	92.1	167,155	6.6	31,150	1.2
1996	2,669,195	1,615	0.1	2,455,075	92.0	178,505	6.7	34,000	1.3
British Columbia									
1951	1,165,210	727	0.1	1,112,937	95.5	39,433	3.4	12,113	1.0
1961	1,629,082	2,559	0.2	1,552,560	95.3	57,504	3.5	16,459	1.0
1971	2,184,625	1,775	0.1	2,054,690	94.1	101,435	4.6	26,725	1.2
1981	2,713,615	1,445	0.0	2,518,965	92.8	154,170	5.7	39,035	1.4
1991	3,247,510	1,140	0.0	2,976,330	91.6	207,175	6.4	62,865	1.9
1996	3,689,750	1,775	0.0	3,342,345	90.6	248,590	6.7	97,040	2.6
Yukon									
1951	9,096	10	0.1	8,337	91.7	519	5.7	230	2.5
1961	14,628	38	0.3	13,679	93.5	825	5.6	86	0.6
1971	18,390	10	0.0	17,130	93.1	1,210	6.6	40	0.2
1981	23,075	10	0.0	21,200	91.9	1,820	7.9	45	0.2
1991	27,655	25	0.1	25,035	90.5	2,570	9.3	25	0.1
1996	30,655	50	0.2	27,340	89.2	3,210	10.5	55	0.2

Knowledge of Official Languages

Table A.3

Population by Knowledge of Official Languages, Canada, Provinces, Territories and Canada less Quebec, 1951 to 1996

Total		Knowledge of Official Languages							
		French Only		English Only		French and English		Neither French, nor English	
		Number	%	Number	%	Number	%	Number	%
Northwest Territories									
1951	16,004	171	1.1	6,929	43.3	1,031	6.4	7,873	49.2
1961	22,998	109	0.5	13,554	58.9	1,614	7.0	7,721	33.6
1971	34,805	100	0.3	25,000	73.3	2,120	6.1	7,085	20.4
1981	45,545	60	0.1	36,385	79.9	2,755	6.0	6,435	13.9
1991	57,435	80	0.1	48,855	85.1	3,495	6.1	5,005	8.7
1996	64,125	40	0.6	55,880	87.1	4,035	6.3	4,170	6.5
Canada less Quebec									
1951	9,953,748	207,570	2.1	8,924,582	89.7	689,317	6.9	132,279	1.3
1961	12,979,036	235,016	1.8	11,676,127	90.0	892,294	6.9	175,599	1.4
1971	15,540,545	211,240	1.4	13,837,025	89.0	1,236,365	8.0	255,915	1.6
1981	17,714,430	160,640	0.9	15,696,655	88.6	1,616,855	9.1	240,280	1.4
1991	20,183,735	151,370	0.7	17,733,005	87.9	1,985,670	9.8	313,690	1.6
1996	21,483,025	127,370	0.6	18,775,740	87.3	2,180,720	10.2	399,195	1.9

Note: Since the 1981 Census, the figures exclude institutional residents, which represent approximately 1% of the population.

Sources: Census of Canada, 1951, 1961, 1971, 1981, 1991 and 1996.

Table A.4
Population by First Official Language Spoken, Canada, Provinces, Territories and Canada less Quebec, 1991 and 1996

| | Total | First Official Language Spoken | | | | Official Language Minority(1) | |
| | | French | English | French and English | Neither French, nor English | | |
		Number	Number	Number	Number	Number	%
Canada							
1991	26,994,035	6,704,675	19,709,370	217,080	362,910	6,813,220	25.2
1996	28,528,125	6,890,880	20,921,770	254,350	461,125	7,018,050	24.6
Newfoundland							
1991	563,940	2,630	560,485	95	725	2,675	0.5
1996	547,160	2,185	544,360	185	435	2,270	0.4
Prince Edward Island							
1991	128,100	5,235	122,720	85	55	5,280	4.1
1996	132,855	5,270	127,425	120	30	5,335	4.0
Nova Scotia							
1991	890,950	35,470	853,680	835	970	35,885	4.0
1996	899,970	34,090	863,720	1,040	1,115	34,615	3.8
New Brunswick							
1991	716,495	241,765	472,550	1,730	455	242,630	33.9
1996	729,630	240,060	487,200	1,965	405	241,040	33.0

Table A.4

Population by First Official Language Spoken, Canada, Provinces, Territories and Canada less Quebec, 1991 and 1996

	Total	First Official Language Spoken					
		French	English	French and English	Neither French, nor English.	Official Language Minority (1)	
		Number	Number	Number	Number	Number	%
Quebec							
1991	6,810,300	5,772,180	832,045	144,505	61,565	904,305	13.3
1996	7,045,085	5,963,675	842,105	167,460	71,845	925,835	13.1
Ontario							
1991	9,977,050	483,445	9,255,865	52,410	185,335	509,650	5.1
1996	10,642,790	480,650	9,860,780	62,300	239,060	511,800	4.8
Manitoba							
1991	1,079,395	46,665	1,017,500	2,265	12,965	47,800	4.4
1996	1,100,290	45,570	1,041,230	2,010	11,490	46,570	4.2
Saskatchewan							
1991	976,040	19,315	950,350	975	5,395	19,805	2.0
1996	976,615	17,310	953,775	810	4,720	17,720	1.8
Alberta							
1991	2,519,180	50,565	2,433,560	5,430	29,635	53,280	2.1
1996	2,669,195	49,390	2,580,675	6,220	32,910	52,500	2.0

Table A.4
Population by First Official Language Spoken, Canada, Provinces, Territories and Canada less Quebec, 1991 and 1996

	Total	First Official Language Spoken				Official Language Minority(1)	
		French	English	French and English	Neither French, nor English		
	Number	Number	Number	Number	Number	Number	%
British Columbia							
1991	3,247,505	45,225	3,132,795	8,635	60,850	49,545	1.5
1996	3,689,755	50,285	3,532,485	12,040	94,945	56,310	1.5
Yukon							
1991	27,660	835	26,765	30	25	850	3.1
1996	30,655	1,080	29,455	70	45	1,115	3.6
Northwest Territories							
1991	57,435	1,345	51,055	90	4,935	1,390	2.4
1996	64,120	1,315	58,565	120	4,120	1,375	2.1
Canada less Quebec							
1991	20,183,735	932,495	18,877,325	72,575	301,345	968,785	4.8
1996	21,483,040	927,205	20,079,665	86,890	389,280	970,650	4.5

(1) English is the minority first official language spoken in Quebec, which includes all those with English as a first official language spoken and half of those with both French and English. French is the minority first official language spoken in Canada and in each of the provinces and territories outside Quebec, which includes all those with French as a first official language spoken and half of those with both French and English.

Sources: Census of Canada, 1991 and 1996.

Tableau 4.3 Bilinguisme français-anglais, régions métropolitaines de recensement, 1991 et 1996

Région métropolitaine de recensement[1]	1991 Effectif (en milliers)	%	1996 Effectif (en milliers)	%
Calgary	52,4	7,0	59,9	7,3
Chicoutimi–Jonquière	24,0	15,1	27,6	17,4
Edmonton	64,0	7,7	63,8	7,5
Halifax	30,5	9,6	35,3	10,7
Hamilton	39,0	6,6	41,7	6,8
Kitchener	23,7	6,7	26,0	6,9
London	24,1	6,4	26,1	6,6
Montréal	1 514,4	47,7	1 634,8	49,7
Oshawa	15,7	6,6	17,8	6,7
Ottawa–Hull	398,9	42,8	440,8	44,0
Ottawa–Hull-Qué.	134,7	59,8	152,4	62,1
Ottawa–Hull-Ont.	264,2	37,4	288,4	38,2
Québec	176,4	27,7	199,3	30,0
Regina	10,6	5,6	10,7	5,6
Saint John (N.–B.)	13,1	10,6	15,2	12,2
Saskatoon	13,2	6,3	14,2	6,6
Sherbrooke	50,2	36,4	56,5	39,1
St. Catharines–Niagara	28,9	8,0	30,3	8,2
St. John's (Terre–Neuve)	7,9	4,7	9,3	5,4
Sudbury	60,0	38,5	63,7	40,1
Thunder Bay	8,3	6,8	9,3	7,4
Toronto	309,7	8,0	339,5	8,0
Trois–Rivières	29,1	21,6	33,6	24,4
Vancouver	114,2	7,2	133,5	7,4
Victoria	21,8	7,7	25,9	8,6
Windsor	27,7	10,7	29,0	10,5
Winnipeg	68,3	10,4	71,8	10,9

Sources : Recensement du Canada de 1991 (totalisations non publiées) et 1996.

Le taux de bilinguisme des personnes dont la langue maternelle n'était ni le français ni l'anglais est demeuré stable de 1991 à 1996. Près de 47 p. cent des allophones qui vivaient au Québec en 1996 étaient bilingues, un taux près de

---

1. Les statistiques pour les régions métropolitaines de recensement sont établies à partir des frontières géographiques de 1996.

neuf fois plus élevé que celui des allophones qui vivaient dans les autres provinces et territoires.

Tableau 4.4 Bilinguisme français-anglais selon la langue maternelle, Canada, Québec et Canada moins le Québec, 1991 et 1996

	1991 Pourcentage	1996 Pourcentage
Canada		
Anglophones	8,5	9,0
Francophones	38,9	41,1
Allophones	11,3	11,3
Québec		
Anglophones	59,4	62,9
Francophones	31,5	34,0
Allophones	46,6	46,8
Canada moins le Québec		
Anglophones	6,4	7,0
Francophones	81,1	83,6
Allophones	5,3	5,4

Sources : Recensement du Canada de 1991 et 1996.

Le taux de bilinguisme des anglophones et des francophones varie aussi considérablement selon le groupe d'âge; cette différence reflète deux modes d'apprentissage différents de la langue seconde. Dans le cas des francophones du Québec, le taux atteint un sommet aux âges qui correspondent à une forte participation au marché du travail. Ainsi, on enregistre le taux le plus élevé (48 p. cent) pour le groupe d'âge des 20 à 24 ans et ce taux reste élevé pour les groupes d'âge subséquents.

Chez les anglophones des autres provinces et territoires, on enregistre le taux de bilinguisme le plus élevé aux âges correspondant aux années de fréquentation scolaire. Le taux atteint un sommet (16 p. cent) pour le groupe d'âge des 15 à 19 ans, puis il diminue par la suite. Le taux de bilinguisme plus faible au sein des groupes d'âge plus élevé s'explique notamment par la popularité moindre ou encore l'inexistence des programmes d'immersion en français durant leurs années de fréquentation scolaire. Dans le cas des cohortes plus récentes, dès la maternelle, les enfants avaient l'occasion de s'inscrire à des programmes d'immersion en français ou de suivre des cours de français. Depuis 1971, un nombre de plus en plus grand d'écoles de langue anglaise offrent des programmes d'immersion en français et le nombre d'étudiants inscrits à ces programmes a progressé de façon continue au fil des ans. En d'autres termes, les

anglophones font l'apprentissage du français comme langue seconde principalement à l'école.

Tableau 4.5 Bilinguisme français-anglais selon le groupe d'âge, chez les francophones du Québec et chez les anglophones des autres provinces et territoires, 1996

Groupe d'âge	Francophones du Québec Pourcentage	Anglophones des autres provinces et territoires Pourcentage
Total	33,7	6,8
0 à 4	3,6	1,0
5 à 9	5,6	5,8
10 à 14	13,6	12,9
15 à 19	35,4	16,3
20 à 24	48,2	12,3
25 à 34	46,0	7,0
35 à 44	40,9	5,6
45 à 54	41,5	5,7
55 à 64	35,6	3,7
65 ans et plus	30,7	2,4

Source : Recensement du Canada de 1996, totalisations non publiées.

À l'extérieur du Québec, entre 1981 et 1996, le nombre d'élèves du primaire ou du secondaire inscrits à des programmes d'immersion en français est passé de 65 000 à 273 000, leur proportion au sein des effectifs scolaires admissibles augmentant de 2 p. cent à 7 p. cent. L'Ontario comptait plus de la moitié (55 p. cent) des étudiants inscrits à un tel programme, alors que le Nouveau-Brunswick affichait la plus forte proportion d'élèves au sein de ces programmes.

Au Québec, les programmes d'immersion en anglais pour les francophones sont pratiquement inexistants. Dans le programme régulier, les cours d'anglais sont obligatoires à partir de la quatrième année du primaire. Les exigences du marché du travail jouent sans doute un rôle déterminant dans l'apprentissage de l'anglais comme langue seconde. Entre 1971 et 1996, le taux d'activité de la population du Québec a connu une progression considérable, passant de 53 p. cent à 64 p. cent par suite d'une présence accrue des femmes au sein de la population active. Ce phénomène a probablement eu une incidence directe sur la

progression du bilinguisme, quand on sait que près de la moitié de la population active de la province est bilingue. En 1996, au sein de la population active, 47 p. cent des Québécoises étaient bilingues, contre 38 p. cent en 1971. Il s'agit d'une progression supérieure à celle observée dans la population masculine, au sein de laquelle le taux de bilinguisme est passé de 46 p. cent à 52 p. cent.

Tableau 4.6 Effectifs des programmes d'immersion en français dans les écoles publiques, provinces (à l'exception du Québec) et territoires, 1980-1981, 1990-1991 et 1995-1996

| | Clientèle scolaire potentielle[1] | | | Programmes d'immersion en français | | | | | |
| | 1980-1981 | 1990-1991 | 1995-1996 | 1980-1981 | | 1990-1991 | | 1995-1996 | |
	Effectif	Effectif	Effectif	Effectif	%	Effectif	%	Effectif	%
Total[2]	3 126 091	3 646 680	3 899 657	64 761	2,1	249 523	6,8	272 660	7,0
Terre-Neuve	148 408	126 772	110 161	392	0,3	4 269	3,4	5 074	4,6
Î.-P.-É.	26 296	23 835	23 757	1 280	4,9	3 371	14,1	3 385	14,2
Nouvelle-Écosse	180 384	162 232	159 882	590	0,3	5 286	3,3	10 916	6,8
N.-B.	103 487	88 429	90 708	5 532	5,4	16 693	18,9	16 052	17,7
Ontario	1 739 327	1 837 082	2 001 132	46 638	2,7	133 906	7,3	151 017	7,5
Manitoba	197 894	192 122	189 805	4 286	2,2	19 604	10,2	19 020	10,0
Saskatchewan	203 652	197 857	195 994	1 603	0,8	10 713	5,4	10 404	5,3
Alberta[3]	—	481 338	513 122	—	—	26 924	5,6	26 676	5,2
C.-B.	509 146	517 788	591 531	4 368	0,9	27 984	5,4	29 184	4,9
Yukon	4 925	5 209	6 019	35	0,7	369	7,1	452	7,5
T.N.-O.	12 572	14 016	17 546	37	0,3	404	2,9	480	2,7

– (Nombres non disponibles.)

Source : Statistique Canada, Langue de la minorité et langue seconde dans l'enseignement, niveaux élémentaire et secondaire, 1995-1996, totalisations non publiées.

1. La clientèle scolaire potentielle pour l'ensemble des programmes d'enseignement de la langue seconde correspond à la différence entre le total des effectifs scolaires et les effectifs des programmes d'enseignement dans la langue de la minorité. Pour la période 1980-1981, les données de l'Alberta ne sont pas connues.

2. À l'exclusion du Québec.

3. En Alberta, on dispose de données sur les programmes d'immersion en français uniquement à compter de l'année scolaire 1983-1984. Le nombre d'élèves s'élevait alors à 14 523, soit 3,2 p. cent de la clientèle scolaire potentielle.

Population ne parlant ni le français ni l'anglais

Le nombre de Canadiens ne pouvant parler ni le français ni l'anglais a continué sa progression au cours de la première moitié des années quatre-vingt-dix. Selon les données du recensement de 1996, 473 000 personnes (2 p. cent) ne parlaient aucune des deux langues officielles. Ce chiffre englobe les enfants en bas âge ne pouvant parler aucune langue; mais même si on exclut les enfants de moins de cinq ans, le nombre de personnes ne pouvant parler ni le français ni l'anglais s'élève encore à 386 000.

Tableau 4.7 Population âgée de cinq ans et plus ne parlant ni le français ni l'anglais, provinces et territoires, 1996

	Effectif	%
Ontario	206 550	53,5
Colombie-Britannique	81 955	21,2
Québec	53 245	13,8
Alberta	27 015	7,0
Manitoba	8 885	2,3
Saskatchewan	3 315	0,9
Territoires du Nord-ouest	2 965	0,8
Nouvelle-Écosse	910	0,2
Terre-Neuve	445	0,1
Nouveau-Brunswick	420	0,1
Yukon	50	0,0
Île-du-Prince-Édouard	30	0,0
Canada	385 785	100,0

Source : Recensement du Canada de 1996, totalisations non publiées.

La majorité des personnes ne pouvant parler ni le français ni l'anglais vivent en Ontario, en Colombie-Britannique, au Québec et en Alberta. Ces provinces ont constitué des destinations de prédilection pour nombre des immigrants récents, sous-population au sein de laquelle de nombreuses personnes ne parlent ni le français ni l'anglais. Le nombre des personnes ne parlant aucune des deux langues officielles est beaucoup moins élevé dans les autres provinces et territoires, s'échelonnant de 9 000 environ au Manitoba à moins de 50 à l'Île-du-Prince-Édouard et au Yukon.

En 1996, la majorité des personnes âgées de cinq ans et plus ne pouvant parler aucune des deux langues officielles vivaient dans les grands centres urbains.

Toronto, agglomération dont plus de 40 p. cent de la population est née à l'extérieur du Canada, vient en tête de liste à cet égard (164 000), suivie de Vancouver (72 000) et de Montréal (47 000). Edmonton et Calgary, les deux principales régions métropolitaines de l'Alberta, comptaient chacune environ 12 000 personnes ne pouvant parler ni le français ni l'anglais.

Au cours du premier lustre des années quatre-vingt-dix, le nombre de personnes ne pouvant parler ni le français ni l'anglais a augmenté de façon considérable en Colombie-Britannique et en Ontario, de même que dans les principaux centres urbains. À Toronto, par exemple, le nombre de ces personnes est passé de 124 000 en 1991 à 164 000 en 1996, alors qu'à Vancouver leur nombre était plus d'une fois et demie celui de 1991. L'effectif de ce groupe a aussi augmenté de façon considérable à Calgary, et de façon moins marquée à Montréal. De telles hausses ont de nombreuses implications sur le plan des services scolaires (p. ex., la formation linguistique) et des services sociaux nécessaires pour assurer l'intégration de cette population dans la société canadienne.

Les personnes de langue maternelle chinoise, italienne ou portugaise comptent ensemble pour plus de la moitié (55 p. cent) des Canadiens ne pouvant parler ni le français ni l'anglais. C'est le groupe de langue maternelle chinoise, groupe linguistique ayant affiché la croissance la plus rapide au cours des cinq années qui ont précédé le recensement de 1996, qui comportait le plus grand nombre de ces personnes (135 000), suivi des groupes italien (45 000) et portugais (30 000).

Au sein de la plupart des groupes linguistiques, 60 p. cent environ des personnes incapables de parler une langue officielle étaient des femmes. Cet écart entre les sexes sur le plan des compétences linguistiques s'explique entre autres par le plus faible taux d'activité des femmes. Étant plus actifs, non seulement les hommes sont-ils exposés aux langues officielles au travail, mais ils jouissent aussi d'un meilleur accès aux programmes d'enseignement des langues offerts dans leur milieu de travail.

Tableau 4.8 Population âgée de 5 ans et plus ne parlant ni le français ni l'anglais, Canada, provinces et territoires, 1991 et 1996

Canada, provinces et territoires	1991	1996
Canada	308 535	385 785
Terre-Neuve	570	445
Île-du-Prince-Édouard	75	30
Nouvelle-Écosse	750	910
Nouveau-Brunswick	355	420
Québec	48 225	53 245
Ontario	164 395	206 550
Manitoba	9 785	8 885
Saskatchewan	3 800	3 315
Alberta	24 475	27 015
Colombie-Britannique	52 695	81 955
Yukon	30	50
Territoires du Nord–Ouest	3 380	2 965

Sources : Recensement du Canada de 1991et 1996, totalisations non publiées.

Tableau 4.9 Population âgée de 5 ans et plus ne parlant ni le français ni l'anglais, régions métropolitaines de recensement, 1991 et 1996

Région métropolitaine de recensement	1991	1996
Calgary	10 425	12 600
Chicoutimi–Jonquière	10	30
Edmonton	11 165	11 585
Halifax	495	660
Hamilton	7 715	7 790
Kitchener	4 885	5 075
London	3 580	3 400
Montréal	42 265	46 700
Oshawa	1 070	1 030
Ottawa–Hull	7 280	8 645
Québec	515	770
Regina	735	710
Saint John (N.-B.)	120	140
Saskatoon	910	1 00
Sherbrooke	245	275
St. Catharines–Niagara	2 185	2 500
St. John's (Terre–Neuve)	150	140
Sudbury	400	485
Thunder Bay	795	805
Toronto	123 845	163 560
Trois–Rivières	50	55
Vancouver	45 215	72 300
Victoria	1 495	1 940
Windsor	3 210	3 520
Winnipeg	6 800	6 335

Sources : Recensement du Canada de 1991 et 1996, totalisations non publiées.

FACTEURS INFLUANT SUR L'ÉVOLUTION DES GROUPES LINGUISTIQUES

L'évolution de la taille des groupes linguistiques du Canada résulte principalement de facteurs tels que la fécondité et la migration internationale (immigration et émigration) et aussi, à l'échelle des provinces et des territoires, de la migration interprovinciale. Un autre phénomène influe également sur la taille de ces groupes : la transmission de la langue maternelle des parents aux enfants. La transmission de la langue étant fortement influencée par le type de couples duquel les enfants sont issus, endogames ou exogames (selon que les conjoints aient ou non la même langue maternelle), et par la langue qui est le plus souvent parlée à la maison, l'analyse de l'évolution de la taille des groupes linguistiques ne saurait être complète si l'on ne tenait pas compte de phénomènes tels que l'exogamie et les transferts linguistiques.

On peut résumer de la façon suivante les principaux changements survenus dans l'effectif et la proportion de chacun des groupes linguistiques entre 1951 et 1996 :

Les anglophones

Canada

▸ Croissance annuelle moyenne considérable durant la période de quarante-cinq ans, particulièrement au cours des années cinquante (2,9 p. cent) et soixante (2,2 p. cent).

55

▸ Progression moins forte mais néanmoins importante durant les années soixante-dix, quatre-vingt et la première moitié des années quatre-vingt-dix (croissance annuelle moyenne de 1,4 p. cent, 1,0 p. cent et 0,9 p. cent respectivement).

▸ Légère augmentation du pourcentage d'anglophones au sein de la population, de 59 p. cent en 1951 à 60 p. cent en 1996.

Québec

▸ Croissance de la population anglophone durant les deux premières décennies de la période considérée (respectivement de 2,5 p. cent et de 1,3 p. cent annuellement).

▸ Diminution annuelle moyenne de la population anglophone au cours des deux décennies suivantes, de l'ordre de 1,2 p. cent durant les années soixante-dix et de 1,0 p. cent durant les années quatre-vingt. La diminution annuelle moyenne entre 1991 et 1996 (un peu plus de 1/10 de 1 p. cent) a été sept fois moindre qu'entre 1981 et 1991.

▸ Baisse du pourcentage d'anglophones au sein de la population, celui-ci passant de 14 p. cent en 1951 à 9 p. cent en 1996.

Canada moins le Québec

▸ Augmentation annuelle moyenne substantielle au cours des années cinquante (2,9 p. cent), soixante (2,2 p. cent) et soixante-dix (1,6 p. cent), mais moins marquée de 1981 à 1991 (1,1 p. cent) et de 1991 à 1996 (1,0 p. cent).

▸ Légère diminution du pourcentage d'anglophones à l'extérieur du Québec, qui passe de 78 p. cent en 1951 à 77 p. cent en 1996.

Les francophones

Canada

▸ Croissance annuelle moyenne substantielle durant les années cinquante (2,6 p. cent), moins importante durant les années soixante (1,3 p. cent), et beaucoup moins importante au cours des deux

décennies suivantes (0,7 p. cent et 0,6 p. cent respectivement). Au cours du dernier lustre, leur croissance annuelle moyenne n'a été que de 0,5 p. cent.

▸ Diminution du pourcentage de francophones au sein de la population canadienne, celui-ci passant de 29 p. cent en 1951 à 24 p. cent en 1996.

Québec

▸ Augmentation annuelle moyenne substantielle durant les années cinquante (2,8 p. cent), moins importante durant les années soixante (1,4 p. cent).

▸ Progression encore moins marquée au cours des vingt-cinq années subséquentes : 0,8 p. cent durant la période 1971 à 1981 et 0,6 p. cent entre 1981et 1991 et durant le lustre suivant.

▸ Légère diminution du pourcentage de francophones au sein de la population du Québec, celui-ci baissant de 83 p. cent en 1951 à 82 p. cent en 1996.

Canada moins le Québec

▸ Faibles augmentations annuelles moyennes durant les deux premières décennies de la période considérée (1,8 p. cent et 0,9 p. cent respectivement).

▸ Variation presque inexistante durant les années soixante-dix, augmentation annuelle moyenne de 0,6 p. cent durant les années quatre-vingt, et légère baisse de 0,1 p. cent au cours de la première moitié des années quatre-vingt-dix.

▸ Diminution du pourcentage de francophones à l'extérieur du Québec, qui passe de 7 p. cent en 1951 à 4 p. cent en 1996.

Les groupes de langue non officielle

Canada

▸ Croissance annuelle moyenne substantielle durant les années cinquante (4,8 p. cent), mais beaucoup moins importante au cours des deux décennies suivantes (1,4 p. cent et 1,1 p. cent respectivement).

▸ Progression remarquable de un million de personnes de 1981 à 1991 et de 623 000 personnes de 1991 à 1996 seulement. La croissance annuelle moyenne a ainsi été de 3,2 p. cent entre 1981 et 1991 et de 3,0 p. cent entre 1991 et 1996.

▸ Augmentation du pourcentage d'allophones au sein de la population canadienne, qui passe de 12 p. cent en 1951 à 17 p. cent en 1996.

Québec

▸ Progression annuelle moyenne considérable au cours des années cinquante (9,4 p. cent), suivie d'augmentations annuelles moyennes beaucoup plus faibles durant les deux décennies suivantes (2,8 p. cent et 1,3 p. cent respectivement) et d'un accroissement annuel moyen marqué de 4,2 p. cent entre 1981 et 1991 et de 2,8 p. cent entre 1991 et 1996.

▸ Augmentation du pourcentage de Québécois allophones (de 4 p. cent en 1951 à 10 p. cent en 1996).

Canada moins le Québec

▸ Forte croissance annuelle moyenne durant les années cinquante (4,3 p. cent), suivie d'une progression beaucoup moins marquée au cours de chacune des deux décennies suivantes (1,3 p. cent et 1,1 p. cent respectivement).

▸ Très forte progression de la croissance annuelle moyenne depuis 1981 : 3,0 p. cent entre 1981 et 1991 et 3,1 p. cent entre 1991 et 1996.

▸ Augmentation du pourcentage d'allophones à l'extérieur du Québec, qui passe de 15 p. cent en 1951 à 19 p. cent en 1996.

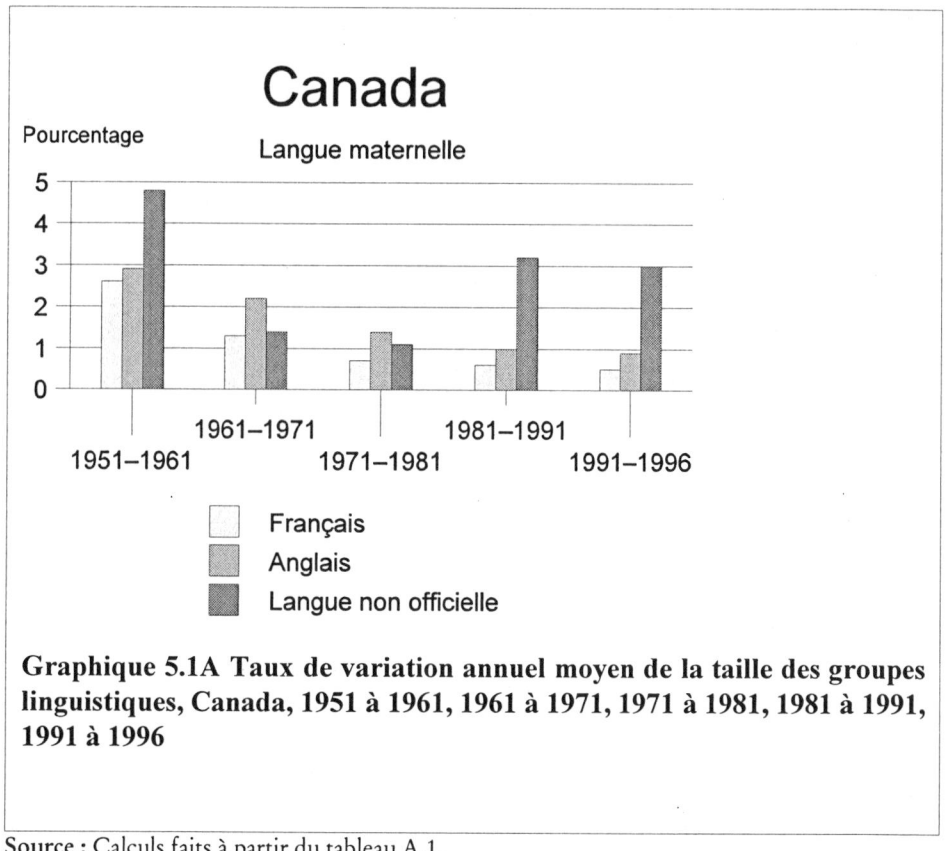

Graphique 5.1A Taux de variation annuel moyen de la taille des groupes linguistiques, Canada, 1951 à 1961, 1961 à 1971, 1971 à 1981, 1981 à 1991, 1991 à 1996

Source : Calculs faits à partir du tableau A.1.

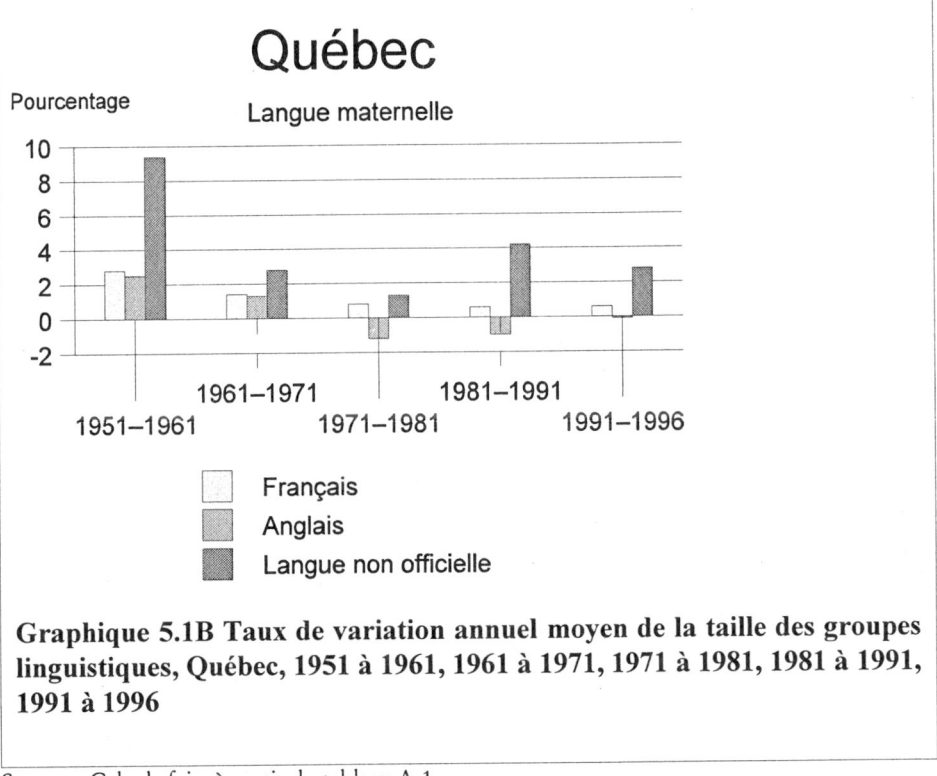

Graphique 5.1B Taux de variation annuel moyen de la taille des groupes linguistiques, Québec, 1951 à 1961, 1961 à 1971, 1971 à 1981, 1981 à 1991, 1991 à 1996

Source : Calculs faits à partir du tableau A.1.

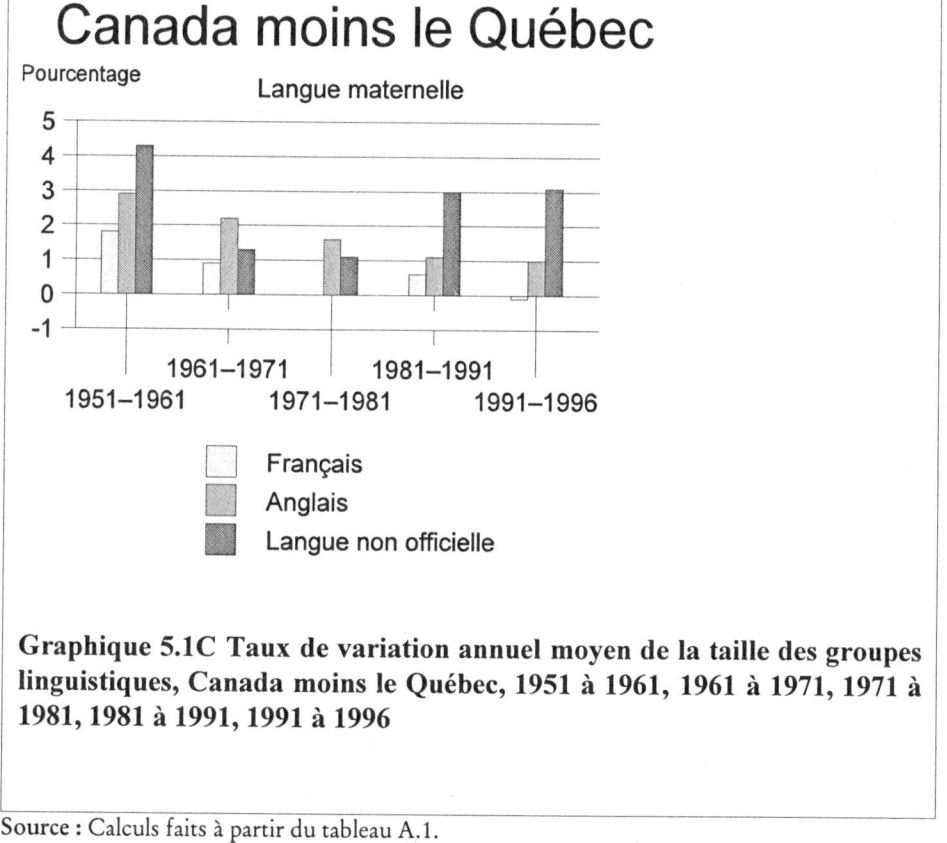

Graphique 5.1C Taux de variation annuel moyen de la taille des groupes linguistiques, Canada moins le Québec, 1951 à 1961, 1961 à 1971, 1971 à 1981, 1981 à 1991, 1991 à 1996

Source : Calculs faits à partir du tableau A.1.

Fécondité

Les différences de fécondité selon la langue maternelle peuvent avoir pour effet de favoriser la croissance d'un groupe en particulier. Telle était la situation dans les années cinquante et au début des années soixante, lorsque les Canadiennes francophones avaient tendance à avoir plus d'enfants que leurs concitoyennes anglophones. Par exemple, pendant la période de cinq ans allant de 1956 à 1961, l'indice synthétique de fécondité s'établissait à 4,3 enfants pour les femmes francophones et à 3,8 enfants pour les femmes anglophones. Le rythme de reproduction plus élevé des francophones leur a permis de maintenir constante leur proportion au sein de la population canadienne, malgré une immigration dont la composition favorisait la croissance de la population de langue maternelle anglaise. Le maintien d'un fort indice de fécondité chez les Canadiennes de langue française constituait le prolongement d'une tendance

ayant existé durant toute la première moitié du XXe siècle. C'est en effet, dans une large mesure, grâce à cette fécondité élevée que la population francophone du Canada a pu maintenir son importance relative autour de 30 p. cent entre 1850 et 1950.

La fécondité des Canadiennes françaises a toutefois fléchi au cours des années soixante, tant et si bien qu'elles avaient tendance à mettre moins d'enfants au monde que les anglophones à la fin de la décennie. Durant la première moitié des années quatre-vingt, les Canadiennes de langue française affichaient un indice de fécondité près de trois fois moindre que celui des années cinquante. Les données historiques indiquent donc une baisse marquée et une convergence de la fécondité chez les Canadiennes françaises et anglaises. Pour la période de 1981 à 1986, l'indice de fécondité a été de 1,5 enfant pour les femmes francophones et de 1,7 enfant pour les femmes anglophones. Alors que les données de la période 1986 à 1991 venaient confirmer cette situation, celles de la période 1991 à 1996 indiquent une réduction de l'écart entre les indices de ces groupes linguistiques en raison du redressement de l'indice des femmes francophones. Les démographes considèrent que le « seuil de remplacement » correspond à un indice de 2,1. Par conséquent, sans la croissance résultant de l'immigration et des transferts linguistiques, les populations francophone et anglophone du Canada verraient toutes deux leur effectif diminuer dans le long terme.

Depuis le milieu des années soixante, les femmes allophones ont affiché un indice de fécondité supérieur à celui des francophones et des anglophones. Il convient toutefois de faire preuve de prudence lorsqu'on évalue l'incidence de cette fécondité plus élevée sur la croissance de l'effectif des groupes allophones. Il arrive souvent que les enfants de ces femmes apprennent une des langues officielles comme langue maternelle.

Tableau 5.1 Indice synthétique de fécondité selon la langue maternelle, Canada, Québec et Canada moins le Québec, 1956 à 1996

	Enfants par femme			
Période quinquennale	Toutes langues	Anglais	Français	Autre
Canada				
1956–1961	3,88	3,80	4,31	3,48
1961–1966	3,51	3,48	3,66	3,40
1966–1971	2,49	2,46	2,36	2,85
1971–1976	1,98	1,95	1,85	2,32
1976–1981	1,75	1,68	1,72	2,11
1981–1986	1,66	1,67	1,49	1,94
1986–1991	1,65	1,68	1,51	1,79
1991–1996	1,69	1,67	1,64	1,85
Québec				
1956–1961	3,99	3,26	4,22	2,79
1961–1966	3,43	3,04	3,54	2,93
1966–1971	2,26	2,09	2,27	2,58
1971–1976	1,82	1,62	1,81	2,26
1976–1981	1,71	1,46	1,71	2,04
1981–1986	1,49	1,46	1,47	1,79
1986–1991	1,51	1,54	1,49	1,78
1991–1996	1,66	1,63	1,64	1,94
Canada moins le Québec				
1956–1961	3,84	3,82	4,95	3,57
1961–1966	3,55	3,50	4,34	3,46
1966–1971	2,58	2,48	2,87	2,89
1971–1976	2,04	1,96	2,12	2,33
1976–1981	1,76	1,69	1,76	2,12
1981–1986	1,72	1,68	1,60	1,96
1986–1991	1,69	1,68	1,56	1,79
1991–1996	1,70	1,68	1,57	1,84

Sources : Lachapelle, R., Évolution des différences de fécondité entre les groupes linguistiques au Canada, Tendances sociales canadiennes, n° 10, automne 1988, no 11-008 F au catalogue, pp. 2–8. Statistique Canada, calculs des auteurs.

Immigration

L'immigration a constitué la principale source d'accroissement de la population allophone. Selon les données du recensement de 1996, 65 p. cent des personnes nées à l'extérieur du Canada (excluant les résidents non permanents) avaient une

langue autre que le français ou l'anglais comme langue maternelle. L'immigration a aussi représenté un important facteur de croissance pour la population anglophone du Canada, mais a eu une incidence beaucoup moins marquée sur l'accroissement de l'effectif du groupe francophone. Parmi la population immigrée ayant déclaré au recensement de 1996 être venue au Canada entre 1951 et 1996, on a relevé un nombre près de neuf fois plus élevé de personnes de langue maternelle anglaise (1,4 million) que de langue maternelle française (159 000). De plus, 86 p. cent des personnes immigrées au Canada durant cette période vivaient à l'extérieur du Québec, dans les provinces et territoires où l'immense majorité d'entre elles apprennent l'anglais et où bon nombre de leurs enfants ont l'anglais comme langue maternelle.

Entre 1951 et 1996, l'immigration a contribué de façon importante à la croissance de la population canadienne. Ainsi, au cours de cette période, l'effectif de la population immigrée est passée de 2 millions à près de 5 millions de personnes. La population immigrée représentait un peu plus de 17 p. cent de la population canadienne en 1996, la plus forte proportion depuis 1951. Chacun des recensements de 1951 à 1991 a vu cette part se maintenir entre 15 p. cent et 16 p. cent. Bien que les taux de croissance de la population immigrée (3,8 p. cent) et de la population née au Canada (2,9 p. cent) aient été remarquables entre 1951 et 1961, c'est entre 1991 et 1996 que l'écart entre les taux de croissance des deux populations a été le plus grand. Avec un accroissement annuel moyen de 2,9 p. cent durant ce lustre, la population immigrée a connu un taux de croissance plus de trois fois supérieur à celui de la population née au Canada (0,8 p. cent).

Tableau 5.2 Taille et proportion de la population immigrée, Canada, 1951 à 1996

	Effectif (en milliers)	Pourcentage
1951	2 060	14,7
1961	2 844	15,6
1971	3 296	15,3
1981	3 867	16,1
1991	4 343	16,1
1996	4 971	17,4

Sources : Recensement du Canada de 1951, 1961, 1971, 1981, 1991 et 1996.

Tableau 5.3 Taux d'accroissement annuel moyen de la population née au Canada et de la population immigrée, Canada, 1951 à 1996

	Née au Canada	Immigrée
1951–1961	2,9	3,8
1961–1971	1,9	1,6
1971–1981	1,1	1,7
1981–1991	1,2	1,2
1991–1996	0,8	2,9

Sources : Recensement du Canada de 1951, 1961, 1971, 1981, 1991, et 1996.

La connaissance des langues officielles est un important facteur qui module l'intégration linguistique des immigrants à la société canadienne. Son importance est elle-même tributaire de la période d'immigration, du pays d'origine et de la langue maternelle des immigrants.

En 1996, au Canada, 75 p. cent de la population immigrée allophone avait déclaré pouvoir soutenir une conversation en anglais seulement, 4 p. cent uniquement en français et 11 p. cent dans ces deux langues. L'examen des données historiques sur la connaissance des langues officielles parmi la population immigrée allophone des trois plus grandes régions métropolitaines de recensement (RMR) permet de constater que, contrairement à Toronto et Vancouver, où la proportion de la population allophone capable de soutenir une conversation en anglais a peu varié depuis 1971 (se situant autour de 80 p. cent), la connaissance des langues officielles a beaucoup évolué à Montréal. Ainsi, alors que 37 p. cent de la population allophone connaissait uniquement l'anglais en 1971, cette proportion se situait à 22 p. cent vingt-cinq ans plus tard. Cette situation s'explique en partie par la forte croissance des allophones ne connaissant que le français (14 p. cent en 1971 comparativement à 25 p. cent en 1996) et par l'augmentation importante de ceux pouvant parler le français et l'anglais (33 p. cent en 1971 comparativement à 44 p. cent en 1996). Ainsi, bien que la proportion des allophones de Montréal déclarant pouvoir soutenir une conversation en anglais (incluant les personnes connaissant le français et l'anglais) a peu varié entre 1971 (70 p. cent) et 1996 (66 p. cent), la proportion de ceux capables de soutenir une conversation en français y a connu une augmentation remarquable, passant de 48 p. cent à 69 p. cent.

Tableau 5.4 Population immigrée allophone selon la connaissance des langues officielles, Montréal, Vancouver et Toronto, 1971 à 1996.

Région et année	Français	Anglais	Français et anglais
Montréal			
1971	14,3	36,7	33,4
1981	19,5	27,6	41,8
1991	24,1	22,4	43,3
1996	24,9	21,5	44,0
Toronto			
1971	0,3	76,1	5,6
1981	0,2	80,2	5,8
1991	0,2	83,0	4,9
1996	0,1	82,4	4,6
Vancouver			
1971	0,1	84,0	5,2
1981	0,1	82,6	5,3
1991	0,1	82,6	4,3
1996	0,1	81,3	3,9

Sources : Recensement du Canada de 1971, 1981, 1991 et 1996.

La situation particulière du Québec transparaît également lorsqu'on regarde l'évolution de la connaissance des langues officielles parmi la population immigrée allophone de la RMR de Montréal. Comme on peut le constater à partir des statistiques du recensement de 1996, plus longue est la durée de présence des immigrants au pays, plus faible est la proportion qui ne connaît que la langue officielle de la majorité, soit le français, et plus forte est celle qui connaît les deux langues officielles. Alors que 18 p. cent de ceux arrivés au pays entre 1951 et 1960 avaient indiqué au recensement de 1996 ne connaître que le français, cette proportion grimpe à 31 p. cent parmi les immigrants récents (ceux arrivés entre 1991 et 1996). Réciproquement, la proportion de la population immigrée qui avait indiqué connaître les deux langues officielles est passée de 47 p. cent parmi ceux arrivés au pays entre 1951 et 1960 à 33 p. cent parmi les immigrants récents. De ce fait, la proportion des locuteurs du français parmi la population immigrée allophone était aussi élevée pour les immigrants récents qu'elle ne l'était pour ceux arrivés au pays entre 1951 et 1960. Dans les régions de Toronto et Vancouver, la situation est différente puisque la proportion de la population immigrée allophone qui avait déclaré ne connaître que la langue officielle de la majorité, soit l'anglais, était plus élevée parmi ceux qui avaient

déclaré au recensement de 1996 être arrivés avant la période 1991 à 1996, alors que la proportion de ceux qui connaissaient les deux langues officielles était peu élevée et plus faible. Ainsi, la proportion de locuteurs de l'anglais parmi la population immigrée allophone était beaucoup plus faible pour les immigrants récents que pour ceux arrivés entre 1951 et 1960, particulièrement à Vancouver.

Tableau 5.5 Population immigrée allophone selon la connaissance des langues officielles et la période d'immigration indiquée au recensement de 1996, Montréal, Toronto et Vancouver.

Région et période d'immigration	Français	Anglais	Français et anglais
Montréal			
1951–1960	17,5	26,9	47,3
1961–1970	18,6	20,2	50,5
1971–1980	25,0	15,1	51,4
1981–1990	29,3	17,0	44,4
1991–1996	31,0	24,7	32,7
Toronto			
1951–1960	0,1	86,2	4,8
1961–1970	0,1	81,8	5,3
1971–1980	1,5	83,1	5,0
1981–1990	1,3	82,2	5,0
1991–1996	0,2	80,3	3,5
Vancouver			
1951–1960	0,1	89,8	5,6
1961–1970	0,0	86,5	5,5
1971–1980	0,1	84,4	4,1
1981–1990	0,1	79,8	4,6
1991–1996	0,7	77,0	2,4

Source : Recensement du Canada de 1996, totalisations non publiées.

En outre, si l'on s'attarde aux immigrants récents allophones établis à Montréal, la proportion de ceux qui connaissent le français est de plus en plus élevée à chaque recensement. Au recensement de 1971, 16 p. cent des immigrants récents allophones avaient indiqué ne connaître que le français. Au recensement de 1981, cette proportion avait plus que doublé (34 p. cent) pour ensuite fluctuer autour de 31 p. cent lors des recensements de 1991 et de 1996. Lorsqu'on inclut ceux qui connaissaient également l'anglais, la proportion des locuteurs du français passe de 41 p. cent pour le recensement de 1971 à 64 p. cent pour celui

de 1996. On observe la même situation dans le cas de Toronto et Vancouver en ce qui concerne la connaissance de l'anglais chez les immigrants récents allophones. Toutefois, à Vancouver, la diminution de la proportion des immigrants récents allophones ayant une connaissance de l'anglais entre 1971 et 1981 est en partie attribuable à l'augmentation notable de la part que représentait les immigrants en provenance de l'Asie. Ceux-ci, contrairement aux immigrants asiatiques venus par la suite, connaissaient l'anglais dans une moindre proportion.

Tableau 5.6 : Population des immigrants récents allophones* selon la connaissance des langues officielles, RMR de Montréal, Toronto et Vancouver, Recensements de 1971, 1981, 1991 et 1996

Région	Français	Anglais	Français et anglais
Montréal			
1971	15,7	31,8	25,0
1981	33,6	19,7	26,3
1991	31,6	22,5	31,9
1996	31,0	24,7	32,7
Toronto			
1971	0,6	64,0	5,1
1981	0.5	68,4	5,2
1991	0,3	80,1	4,0
1996	0,2	80,3	3,5
Vancouver			
1971	0,3	73,4	5,7
1981	0,2	67,5	3,6
1991	0,1	77,5	2,8
1996	0,7	77,0	2,4

*Immigrants arrivés au pays durant les cinq années précédant le recensement
Sources : Recensement du Canada de 1971, 1981, 1991 et 1996.

Partout au pays, l'immigration s'est traduite à court terme par un accroissement de la population de langue maternelle non officielle. L'expérience des immigrants venus au Canada au début du siècle démontre qu'à plus long terme, les descendants des immigrants apprennent souvent l'anglais comme langue maternelle. Les données du recensement montrent qu'à l'extérieur du Québec, 50 p. cent des enfants nés de femmes allophones ayant immigré au pays avant 1981 ont l'anglais comme langue maternelle, comparativement à 13 p. cent de ceux des femmes ayant immigré au pays depuis 1981. Toutefois, la langue

transmise aux enfants est avant tout fonction du pays de naissance de ces derniers. Ainsi, à l'extérieur du Québec, alors que 57 p. cent des enfants nés au Canada de femmes immigrées allophones venues au Canada avant 1981 avaient l'anglais comme langue maternelle, cette proportion n'était que de 16 p. cent chez ceux nés hors du Canada. Parmi les enfants des femmes arrivées au pays depuis 1981, 28 p. cent de ceux nés au Canada avaient l'anglais comme langue maternelle, contre seulement 5 p. cent chez ceux nés à l'extérieur du pays. La proportion des femmes allophones dont les enfants ont le français comme langue maternelle demeure pratiquement inexistante durant les deux périodes.

Au Québec, l'effet de l'immigration à long terme est toutefois plus ambigu que dans le reste du pays : certains enfants issus de femmes immigrées apprennent soit l'anglais soit le français comme langue maternelle. Les enfants de celles venues au Canada avant 1981 ont appris l'anglais (18 p. cent) plus souvent que le français (15 p. cent) comme langue maternelle. Depuis 1981, la situation s'est inversée et les enfants de femmes immigrées apprennent plus souvent le français (11 p. cent) que l'anglais (4 p. cent) comme langue maternelle.

Encore là, on note une différence importante selon le pays de naissance des enfants. En effet, 20 p. cent des enfants nés au Canada de femmes immigrées arrivées avant 1981 avaient l'anglais comme langue maternelle contre 5 p. cent chez ceux nés à l'extérieur du pays. Ces proportions étaient respectivement de 5 p. cent et de 1 p. cent chez les enfants de femmes ayant immigré depuis 1981. À l'opposé, le français était transmis dans une proportion moindre aux enfants nés au Canada de mères venues au pays avant 1981 (17 p. cent) que de mères arrivées depuis 1981 (20 p. cent). Chez les enfants nés hors du pays, ces proportions étaient respectivement de 7 p. cent et de 4 p. cent.

Migration interprovinciale

La langue est un facteur qu'il importe de prendre en considération lorsqu'on étudie la tendance des Canadiens à migrer d'une province à l'autre. Ce facteur est particulièrement important dans le cas du Québec : une migration vers cette province s'identifie fréquemment à un établissement dans un milieu plus francophone et, inversement, une migration hors de cette province correspond souvent à un déplacement vers un milieu plus anglophone. La situation linguistique joue aussi un rôle de premier plan dans la création d'un climat social et culturel, lequel influe sur la propension des Québécois à quitter la province et sur celle du reste des Canadiens à y élire domicile.

Selon les données du recensement de 1996, c'est le Québec qui compte le plus faible pourcentage d'habitants ayant migré récemment depuis une autre province - pourcentage de trois fois inférieur à la moyenne nationale. Tout juste un peu plus de 1 p. cent des habitants du Québec résidaient dans une autre province cinq ans avant le dernier recensement, contre 2 p. cent des habitants de l'Ontario et 3 p. cent ou plus de ceux des autres provinces et territoires.

Alors que la langue constitue pour de nombreux francophones une importante raison pour demeurer au Québec, elle peut avoir pour effet de favoriser les départs au sein de la population anglophone et de faciliter l'intégration des migrants dans le reste du pays. Au cours de la période de vingt-cinq ans ayant précédé le recensement de 1996, environ 400 000 anglophones ont quitté le Québec vers d'autres provinces. Ce chiffre est très élevé, compte tenu du fait que l'effectif de la population anglophone du Québec était de 622 000 personnes en 1996 comparativement à 789 000 en 1971. Durant la même période, les départs francophones s'élevaient à 210 000 personnes (5, 7 millions de francophones ont été dénombrés en 1996 comparativement à 4,9 millions en 1971).

La migration des anglophones hors du Québec a atteint un sommet pendant la période de 1976 à 1981 : environ 130 000 d'entre eux ont quitté le Québec vers d'autres provinces, alors que seulement 25 000 gagnaient la province depuis le reste du pays, pour une perte nette de plus de 100 000 dans la population anglophone. Cette migration a coïncidé avec l'adoption de mesures législatives (Loi 101) visant à promouvoir le statut du français et avec une conjoncture économique favorable dans d'autres grandes provinces. Au cours de la décennie écoulée entre 1986 et 1996, la migration anglophone a fléchi pour se solder par des pertes nettes de 22 000 entre 1986 et 1991 et de 24 000 entre 1991 et 1996 - de loin inférieures à celles enregistrées au cours des trois lustres précédents.

Les Québécois francophones sont pour leur part relativement peu enclins à migrer vers d'autres provinces et la majeure partie de cette migration est compensée par l'arrivée de francophones en provenance d'autres régions du pays. Pendant les vingt-cinq ans qui ont précédé le recensement de 1996, les départs de francophones ont atteint un sommet (environ 50 000 personnes) au cours de la période 1976 – 1981, pour ensuite diminuer. La population francophone du Québec a du reste connu un gain net au titre de la migration interprovinciale au cours des deux dernières périodes quinquennales.

Tableau 5.7 Migration interprovinciale entre le Québec et les autres provinces et territoires selon la langue maternelle, 1971 à 1976, 1976 à 1981, 1981 à 1986, 1986 à 1991 et 1991 à 1996

Période	Total	Anglais	Français	Autre
Du Québec vers les autres provinces				
1971–76	139 500	89 600	39 300	10 800
1976–81	203 000	131 500	49 900	21 600
1981–86	130 200	70 600	45 900	13 700
1986–91	107 500	53 800	37 800	16 000
1991–96	106 300	51 100	33 600	21 600
Total	686 500	396 600	206 300	83 700
Des autres provinces vers le Québec				
1971–76	79 700	39 500	35 210	5 000
1976–81	61 300	25 200	31 900	4 200
1981–86	67 000	29 000	33 000	5 000
1986–91	82 000	31 600	43 000	7 400
1991–96	68 900	26 600	34 800	7 500
Total	358 900	151 900	177 910	29100
Migration nette (arrivées moins les départs)				
1971–76	–59 800	–50 100	–3 890	–5 800
1976–81	–141 700	–106 300	–18 000	–17 400
1981–86	–63 200	–41 600	–12 900	–8 700
1986–91	–25 600	–22 200	5 200	–8 600
1991–96	-37 400	-24 500	1 200	-14 100
Total	-327 600	-244 700	-28 390	-54 600

Sources : Recensement du Canada de 1976, 1981, 1986, 1991 et 1996, données non publiées.
Nota : Population âgée de 5 ans et plus au moment du recensement

Si on examine la destination des anglophones et des francophones ayant quitté le Québec au cours de la période de 1991 à 1996, on constate que leurs schémas de migration diffèrent très peu l'un de l'autre. Une forte majorité de migrants tant francophones qu'anglophones ont opté pour l'Ontario : plus de la moitié dans le premier cas et près des deux tiers dans le second. La Colombie-Britannique est la deuxième destination privilégiée par les deux groupes linguistiques. La province du Nouveau-Brunswick, forte d'une importante minorité francophone (le tiers de la population est de langue maternelle

française) et de sa proximité avec le Québec, a été la troisième destination en importance chez les migrants francophones, alors que l'Alberta est venue au troisième rang pour les migrants anglophones.

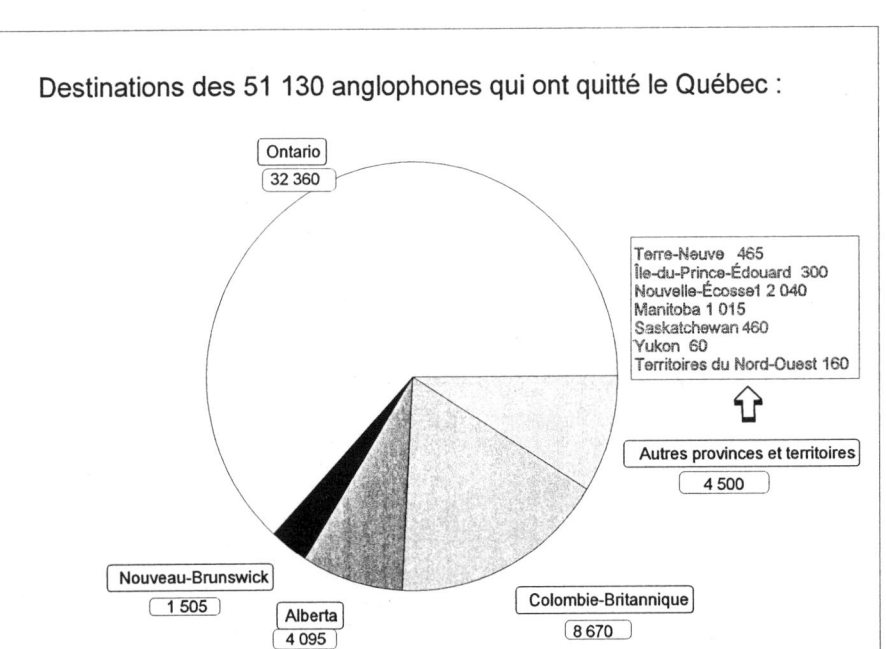

Destinations des 51 130 anglophones qui ont quitté le Québec :

Ontario
32 360

Terre-Neuve 465
Île-du-Prince-Édouard 300
Nouvelle-Écosse1 2 040
Manitoba 1 015
Saskatchewan 460
Yukon 60
Territoires du Nord-Ouest 160

Autres provinces et territoires
4 500

Nouveau-Brunswick
1 505

Alberta
4 095

Colombie-Britannique
8 670

Graphique 5.2A Migration interprovinciale entre le Québec et les autres provinces et territoires selon la langue maternelle, 1991 à 1996

Source : Recensement du Canada de 1996, totalisations non publiées.

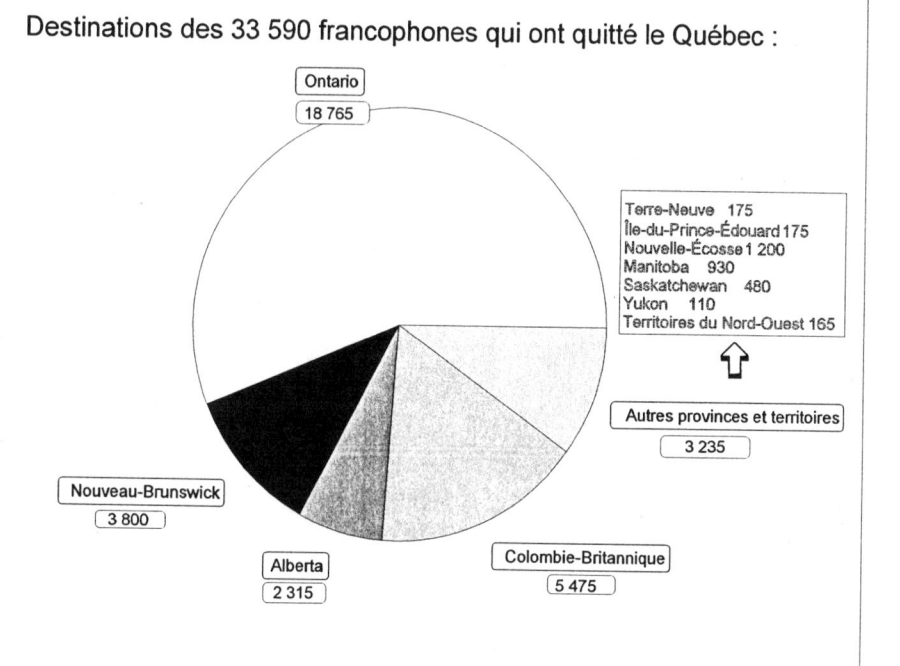

Destinations des 33 590 francophones qui ont quitté le Québec :

Graphique 5.2B Migration interprovinciale entre le Québec et les autres provinces et territoires selon la langue maternelle, 1991 à 1996

Source : Recensement du Canada de 1996, totalisations non publiées.

Lorsqu'on examine l'origine des migrants venus au Québec entre 1991 et 1996, des schémas de migration similaires se dégagent de nouveau. La majorité des migrants francophones (64 p. cent) et des migrants anglophones (65 p. cent) étaient originaires de l'Ontario.

À l'extérieur du Québec, entre 1991 et 1996 le solde migratoire de la population francophone était positif à l'Île-du-Prince-Édouard, en Alberta, en Colombie-Britannique et dans les territoires. En Colombie-Britannique, le solde net s'élevait à 6 200, un nombre considérablement plus élevé que lors de la période quinquennale précédente (3 600). En Ontario, la perte nette de 6 000 était trois fois plus élevée que celle enregistrée au cours du lustre précédent (1 600). À l'opposé, la population francophone du

Nouveau-Brunswick a vu sa perte nette diminuer considérablement entre les deux périodes quinquennales, passant de 1 900 à 500.

Tableau 5.8 Migration interprovinciale des personnes de langue maternelle française, provinces et territoires (à l'exception du Québec), 1986 à 1991 et 1991 à 1996

Provinces et territoires	1986 à 1991			1991 à 1996		
	Entrants	Sortants	Migration Nette	Entrants	Sortants	Migration Nette
T.-N.	600	740	-140	560	890	-330
Î.-P.-É.	555	1150	-595	730	390	340
N.-É.	3 600	4 260	-660	3 400	3 750	-350
N.-B.	7 780	9 650	-1 870	7 330	7 840	-510
Ontario	33 070	34 720	-1 650	24 820	30 860	-6 040
Manitoba	2 540	4 655	-2 115	2 530	3 260	-730
Sask.	1 490	2 825	-1 335	1 520	1 920	-400
Alberta	7 480	8 050	-570	6 570	6 200	370
C.-B.	9 405	5 780	3 625	11 330	5 120	6 210
Yukon	300	255	-45	390	230	160
T.N.-O.	575	530	-40	510	450	60

Source : Recensement du Canada de 1996, totalisations non publiées.

Transmission de la langue

La croissance et le déclin des groupes linguistiques sont aussi fonction de la mesure selon laquelle les membres d'une génération transmettent leur langue à ceux de la génération suivante. On peut étudier ce phénomène en examinant la relation entre la langue maternelle des enfants et celle de leurs parents. En général, lorsque les deux parents ont la même langue officielle comme langue maternelle, les enfants apprennent presque toujours cette langue, que ce soit le français ou l'anglais, comme langue maternelle. Toutefois, lorsque les parents ont une langue non officielle comme langue maternelle, il est fréquent que les enfants apprennent plutôt une des langues officielles (d'ordinaire l'anglais) comme langue maternelle.

La tendance à transmettre une langue à ses enfants varie en fonction d'un certain nombre de facteurs, dont l'un des plus importants est la concentration géographique de la population constituant un groupe linguistique donné. Ainsi, les parents allophones sont plus susceptibles de transmettre leur langue à leurs

enfants s'ils vivent au sein d'une importante communauté ethnique que s'ils sont isolés dans une nombreuse population francophone ou anglophone.

Au Québec, en 1996, 10 p. cent des enfants de moins de 18 ans étaient issus de familles époux-épouse dont les deux parents avaient une langue maternelle non officielle. Environ 10 p. cent de ces enfants ont appris le français comme langue maternelle et un autre 10 p. cent l'anglais. Bien que l'anglais soit transmis aussi souvent que le français, l'usage de cette dernière langue s'est répandu au cours des vingt-cinq dernières années. En 1971, seulement 3 p. cent des enfants dont les deux parents étaient de langue maternelle non officielle apprenaient le français en tant que langue maternelle, alors que 14 p. cent apprenaient l'anglais. Toutefois, les parents allophones du Québec sont toujours plus susceptibles de transmettre une langue non officielle comme langue maternelle à leurs enfants (76 p. cent) qu'ils ne le sont à l'extérieur du Québec (65 p. cent).

Dans le cas des enfants de couples français-anglais, une proportion de plus en plus élevée apprennent le français en tant que langue maternelle tant au Québec qu'à l'extérieur de cette province. Au Québec, le français est maintenant transmis plus souvent que l'anglais en tant que langue maternelle. En 1996, 54 p. cent des enfants apprenaient le français comparativement à 33 p. cent qui apprenaient l'anglais, alors qu'en 1971, on observait la situation inverse : 49 p. cent le français et 51 p. cent l'anglais. De plus, on a observé une augmentation de la transmission de ces deux langues en tant que langues maternelles. Ainsi, en 1996, 12 p. cent des enfants avaient le français et l'anglais en tant que langues maternelles comparativement à 10 p. cent en 1991. Dans les autres provinces et territoires, les progrès du français ont été encore plus marqués au cours des vingt-cinq dernières années. En 1971, 10 p. cent des enfants issus de couples français-anglais apprenaient le français en tant que langue maternelle. En 1996, cette proportion s'établissait à 16 p. cent. En outre, la proportion de ceux qui avaient reçu les deux langues en tant que langues maternelles s'est aussi accrue entre 1991 et 1996, passant de 4 p. cent à 5 p. cent.

Alors qu'en 1996, au Québec, les enfants issus de couples dont les parents appartiennent à la minorité anglophone ont l'anglais en tant que langue maternelle dans 98 p. cent des cas, à l'extérieur du Québec ceux issus de parents francophones ont reçu le français dans 93 p. cent des cas. Il y a eu malgré tout amélioration de la situation des francophones à l'extérieur du Québec au cours des vingt-cinq dernières années puisqu'en 1971, 90 p. cent des enfants avaient appris le français en tant que langue maternelle.

Tableau 5.9 Langue maternelle des enfants de moins de 18 ans vivant dans une famille époux-épouse selon la langue maternelle des parents, Québec, 1971, 1991 et 1996

Québec	Langue maternelle des enfants									
	Anglais		Français		Non officielle		Français et anglais		Autres multiples	
	Effectif	%	Effectif	%	Effectif	%	Effectif	%	Effectif	%
1971- Langue maternelle des parents										
Les deux anglais	164 320	99,1	1 265	0,8	185	0,1	...	...	...	...
Les deux français	5 575	0,4	1 558 785	99,6	905	0,1	...	...	...	...
Les deux non officielle	15 425	14,1	3 120	2,9	90 545	83,0	...	...	...	...
L'un français l'autre anglais	34 790	50,6	33 715	49,1	225	0,3	...	...	...	...
L'un français l'autre non officielle	3 180	17,5	13 560	74,6	1 435	7,9	...	...	...	...
L'un anglais l'autre non officielle	11 965	93,4	195	1,5	650	5,1	...	...	...	...
1991- Langue maternelle des parents										
Les deux anglais	63 540	98,3	725	1,1	135	0,2	240	0,4	20	0,0
Les deux français	1 920	0,2	1 063 545	99,7	470	0,0	575	0,1	185	0,0
Les deux non officielle	12 225	10,5	11 200	9,6	89 220	76,5	260	0,2	3 760	3,2
L'un français l'autre anglais	20 070	36,2	29 535	53,3	120	0,2	5 625	10,2	55	0,1
L'un français l'autre non officielle	2 825	9,7	21 960	75,6	2 400	8,3	735	2,5	1 115	3,8
L'un anglais l'autre non officielle	12 855	87,3	465	3,2	1 065	7,2	110	0,7	225	1,5
1996- Langue maternelle des parents										
Les deux anglais	61 230	97,6	795	1,3	205	0,3	400	0,6	75	0,1
Les deux français	1 935	0,2	1 032 285	99,6	675	0,1	765	0,1	320	0,0
Les deux non officielle	12 555	9,7	12 630	9,8	98 770	76,3	575	0,4	4 990	3,9
L'un français l'autre anglais	19 040	33,4	30 725	53,9	50	0,1	7 130	12,5	55	0,1
L'un français l'autre non officielle	3 260	10,9	21 980	73,7	2 085	7,0	1 035	3,5	1 480	5,0
L'un anglais l'autre non officielle	13 510	85,0	500	3,1	1 300	8,2	165	1,0	425	2,7

Sources : Recensement du Canada de 1971, 1991 et 1996, totalisations non publiées.

Tableau 5.10 Langue maternelle des enfants de moins de 18 ans vivant dans une famille époux-épouse selon la langue maternelle des parents, Canada moins le Québec, 1971, 1991 et 1996

Canada moins le Québec

	Langue maternelle des enfants									
	Anglais		Français		Non officielle		Français et anglais		Autres multiples	
	Effectif	%	Effectif	%	Effectif	%	Effectif	%	Effectif	%
1971 - Langue maternelle des parents										
Les deux anglais	3 299 665	99,9	1 725	0,1	2 460	0,1	...	...	...	...
Les deux français	27 205	9,8	249 735	90,1	185	0,1	...	...	...	...
Les deux non officielle	364 690	44,4	880	0,1	456 580	55,5	...	...	...	...
L'un français l'autre anglais	154 795	90,5	16 175	9,5	145	0,1	...	...	...	...
L'un français l'autre non officielle	25 915	76,8	5 090	15,1	2 735	8,1	...	...	...	...
L'un anglais l'autre non officielle	309 435	97,5	310	0,1	7 635	2,4	...	...	...	...
1991 - Langue maternelle des parents										
Les deux anglais	2 855 360	99,9	1 070	0,0	1 305	0,0	1 000	0,0	555	0,0
Les deux français	8 500	6,6	120 065	92,8	60	0,0	775	0,6	5	0,0
Les deux non officielle	238 425	34,8	540	0,1	419 125	61,2	310	0,0	26 480	3,9
L'un français l'autre anglais	129 635	82,4	21 075	13,4	55	0,0	6 565	4,2	0	0,0
L'un français l'autre non officielle	12 185	71,2	3 015	17,6	915	5,3	665	3,9	335	2,0
L'un anglais l'autre non officielle	326 100	96,0	190	0,1	9 700	2,9	175	0,1	3 510	1,0
1996 - Langue maternelle des parents										
Les deux anglais	2 905 725	99,8	1 220	0,0	1 935	0,1	1 315	0,0	975	0,0
Les deux français	7 220	6,5	102 360	92,8	75	0,1	550	0,5	55	0,0
Les deux non officielle	234 540	30,4	1 220	0,2	502 265	65,1	350	0,0	33 255	4,3
L'un français l'autre anglais	121 500	78,9	24 685	16,0	100	0,1	7 770	5,0	20	0,0
L'un français l'autre non officielle	11 070	68,3	3 390	20,9	760	4,7	595	3,7	390	2,4
L'un anglais l'autre non officielle	321 730	95,3	375	0,1	10 290	3,0	195	0,1	4 980	1,5

Sources : Recensement du Canada de 1971, 1991 et 1996, totalisations non publiées.

Transfert linguistique et exogamie

Bien qu'il n'ait pas une incidence directe sur la taille et la croissance des groupes linguistiques, le transfert linguistique, soit la tendance à parler le plus souvent à la maison une langue qui diffère de la langue maternelle, est souvent un signe avant-coureur d'un changement futur. La langue parlée le plus souvent à la maison sera souvent celle transmise aux enfants en tant que langue maternelle.

Le transfert linguistique est un indicateur de la prédominance d'une langue donnée et n'implique pas nécessairement l'abandon de la langue maternelle. Il est donc possible que la langue maternelle soit utilisée à la maison mais moins souvent qu'une autre langue.

Au cours des vingt-cinq dernières années, on a assisté à une augmentation des transferts linguistiques au sein de la minorité francophone à l'extérieur du Québec. En 1971, 30 p. cent des francophones utilisaient une autre langue que le français le plus souvent à la maison, d'ordinaire l'anglais, comparativement à 35 p. cent en 1991 et à 37 p. cent en 1996. Seuls les francophones de la Colombie-Britannique et du Yukon ont connu une baisse de la proportion de leur population ayant effectué un transfert linguistique. Les francophones du Nouveau-Brunswick étaient les moins susceptibles d'effectuer un transfert linguistique. De 1971 à 1996, la proportion de ceux qui avaient déclaré parler une autre langue que le français le plus souvent à la maison a très peu varié, passant de 9 p. cent à 10 p. cent. La minorité anglophone du Québec a, elle aussi, subi une augmentation de la proportion des transferts linguistiques au cours du quart de siècle ayant précédé le recensement de 1996, passant de 8 p. cent à 10 p. cent, mais cette proportion est demeurée relativement stable entre 1991 et 1996.

Dans l'ensemble du pays, la propension des allophones à parler le français ou l'anglais le plus souvent à la maison n'a cessé de diminuer entre 1971 et 1996. En 1971, 47 p. cent des allophones avaient effectué un transfert linguistique vers le français ou l'anglais. En 1991, ce pourcentage avait diminué à environ 44 p. cent et en 1996, à 40 p. cent. Cette baisse est principalement attribuable à une plus forte immigration durant la décennie 1986-1996. Au Québec, la situation différait sensiblement de celle du reste du pays. Une proportion plus faible d'allophones parlaient une autre langue que leur langue maternelle le plus souvent à la maison, 32 p. cent en 1996, et cette proportion avait peu changé depuis 1971. Toutefois, le français attire de plus en plus les allophones. Parmi ceux qui ont effectué un transfert linguistique vers le français ou l'anglais, une

proportion croissante avait adopté le français : 39 p. cent en 1996, contre 37 p. cent en 1991 et 29 p. cent en 1971.

Tableau 5.11 Population parlant le plus souvent à la maison une autre langue que sa langue maternelle, Canada, provinces, territoires et Canada moins le Québec, 1971, 1991 et 1996.

	Langue Maternelle.								
	Anglais			Français			Non officielle		
	1971	1991	1996	1971	1991	1996	1971	1991	1996
	%	%	%	%	%	%	%	%	%
Canada	1,2	0,7	0,7	6,2	6,2	6,2	47,2	43,8	39,7
Terre-neuve	0,1	0,0	0,0	43,5	55,2	60,5	42,1	38,8	39,5
Île-du-Prince-Édouard	0,3	0,1	0,1	43,2	46,8	47,6	69,8	72,1	71,0
Nouvelle-Écosse	0,3	0,1	0,1	34,1	41,7	43,4	56,6	51,1	47,6
Nouveau-Brunswick	0,8	0,9	1,1	8,8	9,7	9,7	51,3	53,1	56,5
Québec	7,5	9,9	10,2	1,6	1,2	1,1	31,9	33,1	32,3
Ontario	1,0	0,5	0,5	30,3	37,2	39,1	40,6	41,7	37,6
Manitoba	1,0	0,3	0,3	37,2	50,3	53,0	52,4	52,9	52,2
Saskatchewan	0,7	0,2	0,1	52,4	67,6	70,8	65,0	64,7	62,8
Alberta	0,6	0,2	0,3	54,1	64,8	68,0	62,2	52,0	48,3
Colombie-Britannique	0,6	0,3	0,3	73,6	73,3	72,2	60,2	47,4	39,6
Yukon	0,5	0,1	0,2	74,4	53,8	53,6	72,3	75,1	68,5
T.N.-O.	1,3	0,7	0,9	53,4	54,2	60,1	20,4	21,7	25,6
Canada moins le Québec	0,8	0,4	0,4	29,8	35,3	36,7	49,6	45,6	40,9

Sources : Recensement du Canada de 1971, 1991 et 1996, totalisations non publiées.

Chez les personnes qui vivent en couple, la langue maternelle du conjoint peut être un motif à l'accomplissement d'un transfert linguistique. Lorsque les deux conjoints ont la même langue maternelle (couple endogame), la langue parlée le plus souvent à la maison sera très souvent la même que la langue maternelle. Par contre, lorsque les conjoints ont des langues maternelles différentes (couple exogame), l'un d'entre eux devra parler une langue différente de sa langue maternelle le plus souvent à la maison. Toutefois, dans la mesure où l'autre conjoint est lui aussi capable de s'exprimer dans les deux langues, il n'est pas exclu que l'autre langue maternelle puisse être utilisée à la maison, bien que moins souvent.

Au Québec, les anglophones vivant en couple ont beaucoup plus souvent que par le passé un conjoint de langue maternelle française : 29 p. cent en 1996 comparativement à 15 p. cent en 1971. En outre, une proportion de plus en plus faible des anglophones au sein de ces couples exogames parlait l'anglais le plus souvent à la maison : 52 p. cent en 1996 comparativement à 62 p. cent en 1971; 85 p. cent des anglophones ayant un conjoint francophone étaient bilingues français-anglais en 1996 comparativement à 75 p. cent en 1971.

À l'extérieur du Québec, les francophones vivant en couple ont de plus en plus souvent un conjoint de langue maternelle anglaise : 36 p. cent en 1996 comparativement à 22 p. cent en 1971. Dans leur cas, la proportion des transferts linguistiques ayant toujours été très élevée (environ 96 p. cent en 1971 et en 1996), l'augmentation de la proportion de couples exogames français-anglais n'est pas pour améliorer la situation du français en tant que langue parlée le plus souvent à la maison. En 1996, 92 p. cent des francophones dans ces couples exogames étaient bilingues français-anglais, alors que cette proportion était de 21 p. cent pour les anglophones.

Dans le cas des allophones, leur effectif étant à la hausse, le phénomène de l'exogamie n'évolue pas aussi rapidement que chez les francophones et les anglophones qui vivent en situation minoritaire. En 1996, tant au Québec qu'à l'extérieur du Québec, plus de 80 p. cent d'entre eux avaient un conjoint dont la langue maternelle était autre que le français ou l'anglais. Au Québec, plus des deux tiers des allophones dans des couples endogames parlaient une langue non officielle le plus souvent à la maison, comparativement à 61 p. cent de ceux à l'extérieur du Québec. Au Québec, les allophones dont le conjoint était anglophone parlaient le plus souvent à la maison l'anglais dans 88 p. cent des cas, alors que ceux dont le conjoint était francophone avaient le français en tant que langue d'usage dans 65 p. cent des cas. Cette situation était comparable à celle observée en 1971. En 1996, parmi les allophones dont le conjoint était soit francophone soit anglophone, environ les trois quarts étaient bilingues français-anglais. En 1971, le taux de bilinguisme des allophones dans les couples allophone-anglophone (50 p. cent) était beaucoup plus faible que dans les couples allophone-francophone (67 p. cent).

Tableau 5.12 A) Bilinguismefrançais-anglaiset utilisation de l'anglais le plus souvent à la maison chez les anglophones vivant en couple selon la langue maternelle du conjoint, Québec, 1971, 1991 et 1996

	Anglophones vivant en couple					
Langue maternelle du conjoint [1]	Total	%	Bilingues français-anglais	%	Utilisant l'anglais le plus souvent à la maison	%
1971						
Total	322 245	100,0	136 390	42,3	295 260	91,6
Anglais	265 010	82,2	96 400	36,4	256 525	96,8
Français	47 185	14,6	35 390	75,0	29 450	62,4
Autre	10 050	3,1	4 600	45,8	9 285	92,4
1991						
Total	255 970	100,0	157 075	61,4	216 425	84,6
Anglais	168 500	65,8	86 795	51,5	163 795	97,2
Français	70 790	27,7	59 295	83,8	37 310	52,7
Autre	16 680	6,5	10 985	65,9	15 320	91,8
1996						
Total	245 245	100,0	159 340	65,0	205 155	83,7
Anglais	157 050	64,0	86 950	55,4	152 415	97,0
Français	71 320	29,1	60 425	84,7	37 145	52,1
Autre	16 870	6,9	11965	70,9	15 595	92,4

Sources : Recensement du Canada de 1971, 1991 et 1996, totalisations non publiées.

1. Seules les réponses uniques aux questions sur la langue maternelle et la langue parlée à la maison ont été utilisées.

Tableau 5.12 B) Bilinguisme français-anglais et utilisation du français le plus souvent à la maison chez les francophones vivant en couple selon la langue maternelle du conjoint, Canada moins le Québec, 1971, 1991 et 1996

Langue maternelle du conjoint [1]	Francophones vivant en couple						
	Total	%	Bilingues français-anglais	%	Utilisant le français le plus souvent à la maison	%
1971						
Total	398 940	100,0	349 100	87,5	255 840	64,1
Anglais	86 580	21,7	89 420	103,3	8 370	9,7
Français	292 320	73,3	239 985	82,1	245 455	84,0
Autre	20 040	5,0	19 695	98,3	2 015	10,1
1991						
Total	511 510	100,0	441 345	86,3	281 375	55,0
Anglais	177 800	35,0	162 260	91,3	15 425	8,7
Français	311 940	61,4	259 875	83,3	263 620	84,5
Autre	21 770	4,3	19 210	88,2	2 330	10,7
1996						
Total	507 660	100,0	447 955	88,2	274 310	54,0
Anglais	184 610	36,4	169 790	92,0	17 465	9,5
Français	300 690	59,2	258 040	85,8	254 125	84,5
Autre	22 360	4,4	20 125	90,0	2 720	12,2

Sources : Recensement du Canada de 1971, 1991 et 1996, totalisations non publiées.

---

1. Seules les réponses uniques aux questions sur la langue maternelle et la langue parlée à la maison ont été utilisées.

Tableau 5.12 C) Bilinguisme français-anglais et utilisation du français le plus souvent à la maison chez les allophones vivant en couple selon la langue maternelle du conjoint, Québec, 1971, 1991 et 1996

Langue maternelle du conjoint[1]	Allophones vivant en couple				Langue utilisée le plus souvent à la maison					
	Total	%	Bilingues français-anglais	%	Français Nombre	%	Anglais Nombre	%	Non officielle Nombre	%
1971										
Total	189 890	100,0	61 915	32,6	17 510	9,2	43 685	23,0	128 690	67,8
Anglais	9 980	5,3	4 970	49,8	265	2,7	8 800	88,2	910	9,1
Français	13 935	7,3	9 325	66,9	8 585	61,6	4 170	29,9	1 180	8,5
Autre	165 975	87,4	47 620	28,7	8 660	5,2	30 715	18,5	126 600	76,3
1991										
Total	294 350	100,0	135 825	46,1	37 295	12,7	64 910	22,1	170 435	57,9
Anglais	16 680	5,7	11 770	70,6	580	3,5	14 580	87,4	670	4,0
Français	32 525	11,0	23 870	73,4	21 035	64,7	6 870	21,1	2 260	6,9
Autre	245 145	83,3	100 185	40,9	15 680	6,4	43 460	17,7	167 505	68,3
1996										
Total	326 360	100,0	154 425	47,3	40 280	12,3	69 035	21,2	191 230	58,6
Anglais	16 870	5,2	12 390	73,4	655	3,9	14 875	88,2	810	4,8
Français	33 875	10,4	25 995	76,7	21 905	64,7	7 430	21,9	1 640	4,8
Autre	275 615	84,5	116 040	42,1	17 720	6,4	46 730	17,0	188 780	68,5

Sources : Recensement du Canada de 1971, 1991 et 1996, totalisations non publiées.

1. Seules les réponses uniques aux questions sur la langue maternelle et la langue parlée à la maison ont été utilisées.

Tableau 5.12 D) Bilinguisme français-anglais et utilisation du français, de l'anglais ou d'une langue non officielle le plus souvent à la maison chez les allophones vivant en couple selon la langue maternelle du conjoint, Canada moins le Québec, 1971, 1991 et 1996

Langue maternelle du conjoint[1]	Total		Bilingues français-anglais		Allophones vivant en couple / Langue utilisée le plus souvent à la maison					
					Français		Anglais		Non officielle	
	Total	%	Nombre	%	Nombre	%	Nombre	%	Nombre	%
1971										
Total	1 365 740	100,0	48 045	3,5	2 885	0,2	707 875	51,8	654 985	48,0
Anglais	211 740	15,5	10 830	5,1	135	0,1	204 310	96,5	7 305	3,4
Français	19 630	1,4	3 720	19,0	1 140	5,8	17 515	89,2	975	5,0
Autre	1 134 370	83,1	33 495	3,0	1 610	0,1	486 050	42,8	646 705	57,0
1991										
Total	1 945 755	100,0	85 835	4,4	2 525	0,1	949 240	48,8	881 150	45,3
Anglais	373 390	19,2	28 120	7,5	145	0,0	357 340	95,7	10 370	2,8
Français	21 760	1,1	5 600	25,7	1 345	6,2	18 635	85,6	995	4,6
Autre	1 550 605	79,7	52 115	3,4	1 035	0,1	573 265	37,0	869 785	56,1
1996										
Total	2 199 345	100,0	96 790	4,4	2 935	0,1	956 385	43,5	1 105 795	50,3
Anglais	384 010	17,5	31 085	8,1	155	0,0	369 760	96,3	8 005	2,1
Français	22 360	1,0	6 210	27,8	1 505	6,7	19 290	86,3	785	3,5
Autre	1 792 975	81,5	59 495	3,3	1 275	0,1	567 335	31,6	1 097 005	61,2

Sources : Recensement du Canada de 1971, 1991 et 1996, totalisations non publiées.

1. Seules les réponses uniques aux questions sur la langue maternelle et la langue parlée à la maison ont été utilisées.

Bilan des facteurs

Malgré l'augmentation de leur nombre au Canada, les francophones ont vu diminuer leur importance relative au sein de la population canadienne de 1951 à 1996. Les deux principaux facteurs qui ont contribué à ce déclin ont été la baisse de l'indice de fécondité des femmes francophones et l'immigration au Canada de nombreuses personnes de langue maternelle autre que française. L'arrivée de ces immigrants est venue grossir considérablement les effectifs de la population anglophone et de la population allophone, mais n'a constitué qu'un apport négligeable pour la population francophone.

Au Québec, le nombre de francophones a connu une progression considérable, mais leur pourcentage au sein de la population a fluctué entre 80 p. cent et 83 p. cent de 1951 à 1996. Le départ de nombreux anglophones a permis à la population francophone de maintenir son importance relative malgré une baisse de l'indice de fécondité des femmes francophones et une croissance de la population allophone, surtout au cours des quinze dernières années.

À l'extérieur du Québec, le nombre de francophones a augmenté, mais leur proportion au sein de la population a diminué sans cesse. Ce recul, qui jusqu'en 1991 était surtout le fait de la croissance de la population non francophone, dont l'effectif s'était accru considérablement sous l'effet de l'immigration, s'explique maintenant aussi par une diminution de leur effectif. Outre la baisse de leur fécondité, la forte tendance des enfants nés de couples français-anglais à apprendre l'anglais comme langue maternelle a contribué à ce fléchissement.

La taille de la population anglophone du Canada a augmenté de façon importante entre 1951 et 1996, alors que leur proportion au sein de la population (60 p. cent en 1996) est demeurée presque inchangée. L'immigration et la tendance des enfants d'immigrants à apprendre l'anglais comme langue maternelle ont fortement contribué à cette augmentation de l'effectif du groupe anglophone. Au Québec, le groupe de langue maternelle anglaise a vu diminuer tant son effectif que sa proportion au sein de la population en raison de la forte migration vers les autres provinces et territoires.

La population allophone a vu s'accroître tant son effectif que sa proportion au sein de la population canadienne. C'est l'immigration qui constitue le principal facteur de croissance pour la plupart des groupes linguistiques autres que les groupes français et anglais, la majeure partie des immigrants ayant une langue non officielle comme langue maternelle.

CONCLUSION

Nous avons assisté au cours des quarante-cinq dernières années, soit de 1951 à 1996, à une modification considérable du profil linguistique du pays. Durant cette période, l'effectif de la population canadienne a plus que doublé, pour passer de quatorze à vingt-neuf millions d'habitants. Il est rare que des progressions de cet ordre prennent place sans avoir un effet sur la composition de la population. La présente étude nous a permis de donner un aperçu des principaux changements survenus au fil des ans et de brosser un tableau de la situation linguistique actuelle.

Les facteurs qui ont contribué à l'établissement de la situation actuelle entre les groupes francophone, anglophone et allophone, soit la fécondité, la migration (internationale et interprovinciale) et la transmission de la langue à la génération suivante, continueront à jouer un rôle de premier plan dans l'évolution future des groupes linguistiques partout au pays. Il est difficile d'imaginer un scénario raisonnable qui pourrait renverser la tendance à la baisse du poids des francophones dans l'ensemble du pays.

Les fluctuations du pourcentage d'allophones au sein de la population canadienne sont tributaires de l'immigration. À court terme, cette dernière provoque un accroissement de l'effectif de cette population, mais, à long terme, les enfants et petits-enfants d'immigrants ont tendance à apprendre une des langues officielles comme langue maternelle. Aussi, une forte immigration pourrait permettre au pourcentage de Canadiens allophones de se maintenir ou même de croître brièvement, mais, pour autant que les tendances observées chez les immigrants se prolongent, leur pourcentage finira par diminuer.

La population de langue maternelle anglaise a vu son effectif augmenter sous l'effet de l'immigration, à la faveur de la venue d'autres anglophones au Canada et de l'adoption de la langue majoritaire en Amérique du Nord par les

descendants des immigrants appartenant à d'autres groupes linguistiques. Bien que l'immigration ait pour effet à court terme de faire croître l'effectif du groupe allophone, elle se traduit à long terme par une augmentation du nombre de Canadiens utilisant l'anglais. Si l'immigration continue de favoriser la croissance du groupe anglophone et que la fécondité des deux groupes de langue officielle se maintient au niveau actuel, il est probable que tant le nombre d'anglophones que leur proportion au sein de la population augmenteront dans l'avenir.

GLOSSAIRE

Langue maternelle	Première langue apprise à la maison dans l'enfance et encore comprise par le recensé au moment du recensement.
Langue parlée à la maison	Langue que le recensé parlait le plus souvent à la maison au moment du recensement.
Connaissance des langues officielles	Indique si le recensé peut soutenir une conversation en français seulement, en anglais seulement, en français et en anglais, ou dans aucune des deux langues officielles du Canada.
Connaissance des langues non officielles	Indique toutes les langues autres que le français ou l'anglais dans lesquelles le recensé peut soutenir une conversation.
Première langue officielle parlée	Indique la langue officielle actuellement parlée qui, dans la plupart des cas, a été apprise en premier lieu par le recensé.
Anglophone	Personne de langue maternelle anglaise.
Francophone	Personne de langue maternelle française.
Allophone	Personne ayant une langue non officielle comme langue maternelle.
Locuteur de l'anglais	Personne pouvant soutenir une conversation en anglais.

Locuteur du français	Personne pouvant soutenir une conversation en français.
Groupe linguistique	Ensemble de personnes ayant la même langue maternelle.
Transfert linguistique	Indique l'utilisation d'une langue autre que la langue maternelle le plus souvent à la maison.
Exogamie	Situation des couples dont les conjoints ont des langues maternelles différentes.

QUALITÉ DES DONNÉES

Les statistiques utilisées dans la présente étude proviennent des données-échantillon des recensements de 1971 à 1996. Pour celui de 1971, elles sont tirées des réponses obtenues auprès d'un tiers des ménages canadiens ayant rempli le questionnaire complet et, depuis le recensement de 1981, de un cinquième. Pour les recensements de 1991 et 1996, en particulier, on considère que les données sur la langue maternelle recueillies auprès de l'échantillon sont plus précises que celles qui ont été recueillies auprès de l'ensemble de la population, puisqu'on relève beaucoup moins de réponses multiples dans le premier cas. Des études d'évaluation ont démontré que le nombre de personnes ayant plus d'une langue maternelle est surestimé dans les ménages ayant rempli le questionnaire abrégé du recensement. La différence dans la proportion de réponses multiples obtenues selon la source utilisée est sans doute attribuable au fait que, dans le questionnaire abrégé, la langue maternelle était la seule question posée alors que, dans le questionnaire détaillé, d'autres questions linguistiques étaient posées avant la question sur la langue maternelle. Les répondants auraient eu moins tendance à déclarer deux langues maternelles ou plus lorsqu'ils pouvaient d'abord faire état de leurs connaissances linguistiques. Toutefois, quelle que soit la base de données utilisée, le sens des tendances est identique dans la plupart des cas.

Depuis le recensement de 1981, les statistiques tirées de la base de données-échantillon (20 p. cent) excluent les pensionnaires d'un établissement institutionnel. Par conséquent, les effectifs pour ce recensement et les recensements suivants sont plus faibles qu'ils ne l'auraient été si cette population avait été incluse, et ne sont donc pas parfaitement comparables avec ceux des recensements antérieurs.

Pour les fins de l'analyse, les réponses multiples ont été réparties également entre les langues déclarées. Par exemple, si un nombre donné de répondants

91

avaient déclaré le français et l'anglais comme langues maternelles ou comme langues parlées à la maison, la moitié des réponses étaient ajoutées à la catégorie « français » et l'autre moitié, à la catégorie « anglais ». La même méthode de répartition a été appliquée dans le cas des réponses multiples faisant état d'une langue officielle et d'une langue non officielle.

Pour la première fois en 1991, les résidents non permanents du Canada ont été inclus dans le champ d'observation du recensement. Font partie de ce groupe les personnes qui sont titulaires d'un permis de séjour pour étudiants, d'un permis de travail ou d'un permis ministériel, ou encore qui revendiquent le statut de réfugié, ainsi que les personnes qui sont à leur charge. Avant 1991, ces personnes étaient considérées comme des résidents étrangers et n'étaient pas dénombrées. Comme bon nombre des résidents non permanents ont une langue non officielle comme langue maternelle, leur inclusion dans le champ d'observation se traduit par un léger gonflement du pourcentage de Canadiens faisant partie de la population allophone en 1991 et en 1996.

TABLEAUX EN ANNEXE

Tableau A.1
Population selon la langue maternelle, Canada, provinces, territoires et Canada moins le Québec, 1951 à 1996

	Total	Langue maternelle					
		Français		Anglais		Langue non officielle	
		Effectif	%	Effectif	%	Effectif	%
Canada							
1951	14 009 429	4 068 850	29,0	8 280 809	59,1	1 659 770	11,8
1961	18 238 247	5 123 151	28,1	10 660 534	58,5	2 454 562	13,5
1971	21 568 310	5 792 710	26,9	12 967 445	60,1	2 808 155	13,0
1981	24 083 505	6 177 795	25,7	14 784 810	61,4	3 120 900	13,0
1991	26 994 040	6 562 065	24,3	16 311 210	60,4	4 120 770	15,3
1996	28 528 130	6 711 644	23,5	17 072 432	59,8	4 744 059	16,6
Terre–Neuve							
1951	361 416	2 321	0,6	357 328	98,9	1 767	0,5
1961	457 853	3 150	0,7	451 530	98,6	3 173	0,7
1971	522 105	3 610	0,7	514 415	98,5	4 080	0,8
1981	563 745	2 580	0,5	557 040	98,8	4 125	0,7
1991	563 925	2 855	0,5	555 925	98,6	5 140	0,9
1996	547 160	2 440	0,4	539 048	98,5	5 663	1,0
Île–du–Prince–Édouard							
1951	98 429	8 477	8,6	89 241	90,7	711	0,7
1961	104 629	7 958	7,6	95 564	91,3	1 107	1,1
1971	111 640	7 360	6,6	103 115	92,4	1 165	1,1
1981	121 220	5 835	4,8	114 095	94,1	1 295	1,1
1991	128 100	5 750	4,5	120 770	94,3	1 585	1,2
1996	132 860	5 722	4,3	125 017	94,1	2 137	1,6

Tableau A.1

Population selon la langue maternelle, Canada, provinces, territoires et Canada moins le Québec, 1951 à 1996

| | Total | Langue maternelle | | | | | |
| | | Français | | Anglais | | Langue non officielle | |
	Effectif	Effectif	%	Effectif	%	Effectif	%
Nouvelle–Écosse							
1951	642 584	38 945	6,1	588 610	91,6	15 029	2,3
1961	737 007	39 568	5,4	680 233	92,3	17 206	2,3
1971	788 960	39 585	5,0	733 195	93,0	16 180	2,1
1981	839 800	35 385	4,2	786 725	93,7	17 695	2,1
1991	890 945	37 525	4,2	831 575	93,3	21 845	2,5
1996	899 970	36 311	4,0	838 283	93,1	25 376	2,8
Nouveau–Brunswick							
1951	515 697	185 110	35,9	325 412	63,1	5 175	1,0
1961	597 936	210 530	35,2	378 633	63,3	8 773	1,5
1971	634 560	214 720	33,8	411 275	64,8	8 565	1,3
1981	689 370	231 970	33,6	448 885	65,1	8 515	1,2
1991	716 500	243 690	34,0	462 875	64,6	9 935	1,4
1996	729 630	242 408	33,2	476 396	65,3	10 826	1,5
Québec							
1951	4 055 681	3 347 030	82,5	558 256	13,8	150 395	3,7
1961	5 259 211	4 269 689	81,2	697 402	13,3	292 120	5,6
1971	6 027 765	4 866 410	80,7	788 830	13,1	372 525	6,2
1981	6 369 055	5 254 195	82,5	693 600	10,9	421 265	6,6
1991	6 810 305	5 585 650	82,0	626 200	9,2	598 455	8,8
1996	7 045 085	5 741 438	81,5	621 858	8,8	681 790	9,7

Tableau A.1
Population selon la langue maternelle, Canada, provinces, territoires et Canada moins le Québec, 1951 à 1996

	Total	Langue maternelle					
		Français		Anglais		Langue non officielle	
		Effectif	%	Effectif	%	Effectif	%
Ontario							
1951	4 597 542	341 502	7,4	3 755 442	81,7	500 598	10,9
1961	6 236 092	425 302	6,8	4 834 623	77,5	976 167	15,7
1971	7 703 110	482 350	6,3	5 967 725	77,5	1 253 035	16,3
1981	8 534 260	465 335	5,5	6 611 990	77,5	1 456 940	17,1
1991	9 977 055	503 345	5,0	7 443 540	74,6	2 030 170	20,3
1996	10 642 790	499 689	4,7	7 777 734	73,1	2 365 367	22,2
Manitoba							
1951	776 541	54 199	7,0	467 892	60,3	254 450	32,8
1961	921 686	60 899	6,6	584 526	63,4	276 260	30,0
1971	988 245	60 485	6,1	662 130	67,0	265 630	26,8
1981	1 013 700	51 620	5,1	731 500	72,2	230 575	22,7
1991	1 079 390	50 775	4,7	793 325	73,5	235 285	21,8
1996	1 100 295	49 100	4,5	822 258	74,7	228 940	20,8
Saskatchewan							
1951	831 728	36 815	4,4	515 873	62,0	279 040	33,5
1961	925 181	36 163	3,9	638 156	69,0	250 862	27,1
1971	926 245	31 795	3,4	685 025	74,0	209 425	22,6
1981	956 445	25 090	2,6	767 110	80,2	164 250	17,2
1991	976 040	21 795	2,2	812 600	83,3	141 645	14,5
1996	976 615	19 901	2,0	823 746	84,3	132 968	13,6

Tableau A.1
Population selon la langue maternelle, Canada, provinces, territoires et Canada moins le Québec, 1951 à 1996

	Total	Français Effectif	%	Langue maternelle Anglais Effectif	%	Langue non officielle Effectif	%
Alberta							
1951	939 501	34 196	3,6	648 413	69,0	256 892	27,3
1961	1 331 944	42 276	3,2	962 319	72,2	327 349	24,6
1971	1 627 875	46 750	2,9	1 262 840	77,6	318 285	19,5
1981	2 213 640	60 605	2,7	1 800 870	81,4	352 165	15,9
1991	2 519 185	56 730	2,3	2 045 905	81,2	416 550	16,5
1996	2 669 195	55 290	2,0	2 175 758	81,5	438 148	16,4
Colombie–Britannique							
1951	1 165 210	19 366	1,7	963 920	82,7	181 924	15,6
1961	1 629 082	26 179	1,6	1 318 498	80,9	284 405	17,5
1971	2 184 625	38 035	1,7	1 807 240	82,7	339 350	15,5
1981	2 713 620	43 415	1,6	2 228 185	82,1	442 025	16,3
1991	3 247 495	51 585	1,6	2 562 240	78,9	633 665	19,5
1996	3 689 755	56 755	1,5	2 809 398	76,1	823 603	22,3
Yukon							
1951	9 096	308	3,4	6 618	72,8	2 170	23,9
1961	14 628	443	3,0	10 869	74,3	3 316	22,7
1971	18 390	450	2,4	15 340	83,4	2 600	14,1
1981	23 080	530	2,3	20 185	87,5	2 365	10,2
1991	27 665	905	3,3	24 550	88,7	2 210	8,0
1996	30 650	1 170	3,8	26 613	86,8	2 868	9,4

Tableau A.1

Population selon la langue maternelle, Canada, provinces, territoires et Canada moins le Québec, 1951 à 1996

	Total	Langue maternelle					
		Français		Anglais		Langue non officielle	
	Effectif	Effectif	%	Effectif	%	Effectif	%
Territoires du Nord–Ouest							
1951	16 004	581	3,6	3 804	23,8	11 619	72,6
1961	22 998	994	4,3	8 181	35,6	13 823	60,1
1971	34 805	1 160	3,3	16 305	46,8	17 340	49,8
1981	45 535	1 225	2,7	24 635	54,1	19 675	43,2
1991	57 435	1 455	2,5	31 705	55,2	24 280	42,3
1996	64 125	1 421	2,2	36 326	56,6	26 378	41,1
Canada moins le Québec							
1951	9 953 748	721 820	7,3	7 722 553	77,6	1 509 375	15,2
1961	12 979 036	853 462	6,6	9 963 132	76,8	2 162 442	16,7
1971	15 540 545	926 400	6,0	12 184 625	78,4	2 429 520	15,7
1981	17 714 450	923 605	5,2	14 091 215	79,5	2 699 635	15,2
1991	20 183 735	976 415	4,8	15 685 005	77,7	3 522 315	17,5
1996	21 483 045	970 207	4,5	16 450 574	76,6	4 062 269	18,9

Nota : À partir du recensement de 1981, les effectifs ne comprennent pas les pensionnaires d'un établissement institutionnel. Ceux-ci représentent environ 1 p. cent de la population.

Sources : Statistique Canada, Recensement du Canada de 1951, 1961, 1971, 1981 1991 et 1996.

Tableau A.2
Population selon la langue parlée à la maison, Canada, provinces, territoires et Canada moins le Québec, 1971 à 1996

Total		Langue parlée à la maison				
	Français		Anglais		Langue non officielle	
	Effectif	%	Effectif	%	Effectif	%
Canada						
1971	21 568 310	5 546 025	25,7	14 446 235	67,0	1 576 050	7,3
1981	24 083 495	5 919 855	24,6	16 375 315	68,0	1 788 325	7,4
1991	26 994 045	6 288 430	23,3	18 440 540	68,3	2 265 075	8,4
1996	28 528 120	6 448 603	22,6	19 294 873	67,6	2 784 643	9,8
Terre-Neuve						
1971	522 100	2 295	0,4	517 210	99,1	2 595	0,5
1981	563 750	1 845	0,3	559 390	99,2	2 515	0,4
1991	563 935	1 340	0,2	559 505	99,2	3 095	0,5
1996	547 155	1 018	0,1	542 628	99,2	3 510	0,6
Île-du-Prince-Édouard						
1971	111 640	4 405	3,9	106 795	95,7	440	0,4
1981	121 230	3 745	3,1	117 040	96,5	450	0,4
1991	128 105	3 050	2,4	124 620	97,3	440	0,3
1996	132 855	3 045	2,3	129 190	97,2	620	0,5
Nouvelle-Écosse						
1971	788 960	27 220	3,5	753 725	95,5	8 015	1,0
1981	839 800	24 435	2,9	806 490	96,0	8 875	1,1
1991	890 945	22 260	2,5	858 130	96,3	10 555	1,2
1996	899 970	20 710	2,3	866 260	96,3	13 000	1,4

Tableau A.2
Population selon la langue parlée à la maison, Canada, provinces, territoires et Canada moins le Québec, 1971 à 1996

	Total	Français Effectif	%	Anglais Effectif	%	Langue non officielle Effectif	%
				Langue parlée à la maison			
Nouveau–Brunswick							
1971	634 560	199 080	31,4	430 720	67,9	4 760	0,8
1981	689 380	216 745	31,4	468 105	67,9	4 530	0,7
1991	716 490	223 265	31,2	488 570	68,2	4 660	0,7
1996	729 625	222 441	30,1	502 526	68,9	4 658	0,6
Québec							
1971	6 027 765	4 870 100	80,8	887 875	14,7	269 790	4,5
1981	6 369 075	5 253 070	82,5	806 785	12,7	309 220	4,9
1991	6 810 300	5 651 795	83,0	761 815	11,2	396 695	5,8
1996	7 045 085	5 830 082	82,8	762 457	10,8	452 547	6,4
Ontario							
1971	7 703 105	352 465	4,6	6 558 060	85,1	792 580	10,3
1981	8 534 270	333 050	3,9	7 310 060	85,7	891 160	10,4
1991	9 977 055	318 705	3,2	8 499 515	85,2	1 158 830	11,6
1996	10 642 790	306 790	2,9	8 900 845	83,6	1 435 155	13,5
Manitoba							
1971	988 245	39 600	4,0	816 560	82,6	132 085	13,4
1981	1 013 705	31 030	3,1	868 295	85,7	114 380	11,3
1991	1 079 395	25 045	2,3	947 090	87,7	107 265	9,9
1996	1 100 295	23 133	2,1	971 608	88,3	105 553	9,6

Tableau A.2
Population selon la langue parlée à la maison, Canada, provinces, territoires et Canada moins le Québec, 1971 à 1996

	Total	Langue parlée à la maison					
		Français		Anglais		Langue non officielle	
		Effectif	%	Effectif	%	Effectif	%
Saskatchewan							
1971	926 240	15 930	1,7	832 515	89,9	77 795	8,4
1981	956 435	10 295	1,1	884 760	92,5	61 380	6,4
1991	976 030	7 155	0,7	921 085	94,4	47 790	4,9
1996	976 615	5 828	0,6	923 443	94,6	47 343	4,8
Alberta							
1971	1 627 870	22 700	1,4	1 477 960	90,8	127 210	7,8
1981	2 213 645	29 690	1,3	2 024 090	91,4	159 860	7,2
1991	2 519 180	20 180	0,8	2 305 200	91,5	193 800	7,7
1996	2 669 195	17 822	0,6	2 432 682	91,1	218 692	8,2
Colombie–Britannique							
1971	2 184 620	11 505	0,5	2 027 120	92,8	145 995	6,7
1981	2 713 620	15 090	0,6	2 479 555	91,4	218 980	8,1
1991	3 247 495	14 555	0,4	2 909 930	89,6	323 010	9,9
1996	3 689 760	16 586	0,4	3 189 883	86,5	483 291	13,1
Yukon							
1971	18 395	135	0,7	17 470	95,0	790	4,3
1981	23 075	240	1,0	22 075	95,7	760	3,3
1991	27 645	390	1,4	26 735	96,7	520	1,9
1996	30 655	543	1,8	29 240	95,4	873	2,9

Tableau A.2
Population selon la langue parlée à la maison, Canada, provinces, territoires et Canada moins le Québec, 1971 à 1996

Total		Langue parlée à la maison					
		Français		Anglais		Langue non officielle	
		Effectif	%	Effectif	%	Effectif	%
Territoires du Nord–Ouest							
1971	34 800	585	1,7	20 225	58,1	13 990	40,2
1981	45 535	630	1,4	28 670	63,0	16 235	35,7
1991	57 435	680	1,2	38 355	66,8	18 400	32,0
1996	64 120	607	0,9	44 112	68,8	19 402	30,3
Canada moins le Québec							
1971	15 540 545	675 925	4,3	13 558 360	87,2	1 306 260	8,4
1981	17 714 420	666 785	3,8	15 568 530	87,9	1 479 105	8,3
1991	20 183 745	636 640	3,2	17 678 730	87,6	1 868 380	9,3
1996	21 483 035	618 522	2,9	18 532 417	86,3	2 332 097	10,9

Nota : À partir du recensement de 1981, les effectifs ne comprennent pas les pensionnaires d'un établissement institutionnel. Ceux-ci représentent environ 1 p. cent de la population.

Sources : Statistique Canada, Recensement du Canada de 1971, 1981 1991 et 1996.

Tableau A.3
Population selon la connaissance des langues officielles, Canada, provinces, territoires et Canada moins le Québec, 1951 à 1996

| | Total | Connaissance des langues officielles | | | | | | | |
| | | Français seulement | | Anglais seulement | | Français et anglais | | Ni français, ni anglais | |
		Effectif	%	Effectif	%	Effectif	%	Effectif	%
Canada									
1951	14 009 429	2 741 812	19,6	9 387 395	67,0	1 727 447	12,3	152 775	1,1
1961	18 238 247	3 489 866	19,1	12 284 762	67,4	2 231 172	12,2	232 447	1,3
1971	21 568 310	3 879 255	18,0	14 469 540	67,1	2 900 155	13,4	319 360	1,5
1981	24 083 495	3 987 245	16,6	16 122 895	66,9	3 681 960	15,3	291 395	1,2
1991	26 994 035	4 110 300	15,2	18 106 760	67,1	4 398 655	16,3	378 320	1,4
1996	28 528 100	4 079 080	14,3	19 134 245	67,1	4 841 310	17,0	473 465	1,7
Terre–Neuve									
1951	361 416	153	0,0	356 377	98,6	3 990	1,1	896	0,2
1961	457 853	522	0,1	450 945	98,5	5 299	1,2	1 087	0,2
1971	522 105	510	0,1	511 620	98,0	9 350	1,8	625	0,1
1981	563 750	145	0,0	550 335	97,6	12 840	2,3	430	0,1
1991	563 940	240	0,0	544 425	96,5	18 495	3,3	780	0,1
1996	547 155	155	0,0	525 190	96,0	21 260	3,9	550	0,1
Île–du–Prince–Édouard									
1951	98 429	914	0,9	88 743	90,2	8 745	8,9	27	0,0
1961	104 629	1 219	1,2	95 296	91,1	7 938	7,6	176	0,2
1971	111 640	680	0,6	101 820	91,2	9 110	8,2	30	0,0
1981	121 225	205	0,2	111 200	91,7	9 780	8,1	40	0,0
1991	128 095	270	0,2	114 795	89,6	12 950	10,1	80	0,1
1996	132 855	170	0,1	118 080	88,9	14 570	11,0	35	0,0

Tableau A.3
Population selon la connaissance des langues officielles, Canada, provinces, territoires et Canada moins le Québec, 1951 à 1996

| | Total | Connaissance des langues officielles | | | | | | | |
| | | Français seulement | | Anglais seulement | | Français et anglais | | Ni français, ni anglais | |
		Effectif	%	Effectif	%	Effectif	%	Effectif	%
Nouvelle-Écosse									
1951	642 584	7 462	1,2	595 257	92,6	39 524	6,2	341	0,0
1961	737 007	5 938	0,8	684 805	92,9	44 987	6,1	1 277	0,2
1971	788 955	4 185	0,5	730 700	92,6	53 035	6,7	1 035	0,1
1981	839 795	1 880	0,2	774 760	92,3	62 350	7,4	805	0,1
1991	890 945	1 580	0,2	811 870	91,1	76 465	8,6	1 030	0,1
1996	899 970	1 375	0,2	813 320	90,4	83 980	9,3	1 295	0,1
Nouveau-Brunswick									
1951	515 697	100 712	19,5	318 560	61,8	96 095	18,6	330	0,1
1961	597 936	112 054	18,7	370 922	62,0	113 495	19,0	1 465	0,2
1971	634 555	100 985	15,9	396 855	62,5	136 115	21,5	600	0,1
1981	689 370	89 340	13,0	417 025	60,5	182 550	26,5	455	0,1
1991	716 495	89 500	12,5	414 955	57,9	211 525	29,5	515	0,1
1996	729 625	73 410	10,1	417 970	57,3	237 765	32,6	480	0,1
Québec									
1951	4 055 681	2 534 242	62,5	462 813	11,4	1 038 130	25,6	20 496	0,5
1961	5 259 211	3 254 850	61,9	608 635	11,6	1 338 878	25,5	56 848	1,1
1971	6 027 765	3 668 015	60,9	632 515	10,5	1 663 790	27,6	63 445	1,1
1981	6 369 065	3 826 605	60,1	426 240	6,7	2 065 105	32,4	51 115	0,8
1991	6 810 300	3 958 930	58,1	373 755	5,5	2 412 985	35,4	64 630	0,9
1996	7 045 075	3 951 710	56,1	358 505	5,1	2 660 590	37,8	74 270	1,1

Tableau A.3

Population selon la connaissance des langues officielles, Canada, provinces, territoires et Canada moins le Québec, 1951 à 1996

Total		Connaissance des langues officielles							
		Français seulement		Anglais seulement		Français et anglais		Ni français, ni anglais	
		Effectif	%	Effectif	%	Effectif	%	Effectif	%
Ontario									
1951	4 597 542	78 974	1,7	4 115 584	89,5	359 965	7,8	43 019	0,9
1961	6 236 092	95 236	1,5	5 548 766	89,0	493 270	7,9	98 820	1,6
1971	7 703 100	92 845	1,2	6 724 100	87,3	716 065	9,3	170 090	2,2
1981	8 534 265	60 535	0,7	7 401 070	86,7	924 475	10,8	148 185	1,7
1991	9 977 055	54 245	0,5	8 593 635	86,1	1 136 245	11,4	192 930	1,9
1996	10 642 785	46 940	0,4	9 116 165	85,7	1 234 895	11,6	244 785	2,3
Manitoba									
1951	776 541	7 869	1,0	685 914	88,3	58 441	7,5	24 317	3,1
1961	921 686	7 954	0,9	825 955	89,6	68 368	7,4	19 409	2,1
1971	988 255	5 020	0,5	881 715	89,2	80 935	8,2	20 585	2,1
1981	1 013 710	2 620	0,3	915 760	90,3	79 990	7,9	15 340	1,5
1991	1 079 390	1 905	0,2	965 100	89,4	98 800	9,2	13 585	1,3
1996	1 100 295	1 495	0,1	983 820	89,4	103 140	9,4	11 840	1,1
Saskatchewan									
1951	831 728	4 656	0,6	767 248	92,2	40 789	4,9	19 035	2,3
1961	925 181	3 853	0,4	865 821	93,6	42 074	4,5	13 433	1,5
1971	926 235	1 825	0,2	867 315	93,6	45 985	5,0	11 110	1,2
1981	956 435	705	0,1	904 900	94,6	43 650	4,6	7 180	0,8
1991	976 035	450	0,0	919 070	94,2	50 800	5,2	5 715	0,6
1996	976 615	345	0,0	920 555	94,3	50 770	5,2	4 945	0,5

Tableau A.3
Population selon la connaissance des langues officielles, Canada, provinces, territoires et Canada moins le Québec, 1951 à 1996

| | Total | Connaissance des langues officielles | | | | | | | |
| | | Français seulement | | Anglais seulement | | Français et anglais | | Ni français, ni anglais | |
		Effectif	%	Effectif	%	Effectif	%	Effectif	%
Alberta									
1951	939 501	5 922	0,6	868 696	92,5	40 785	4,3	24 098	2,6
1961	1 331 944	5 534	0,4	1 253 824	94,1	56 920	4,3	15 666	1,2
1971	1 627 875	3 310	0,2	1 525 575	93,7	81 000	5,0	17 990	1,1
1981	2 213 650	3 700	0,2	2 045 060	92,4	142 465	6,4	22 425	1,0
1991	2 519 180	1 940	0,1	2 318 935	92,1	167 155	6,6	31 150	1,2
1996	2 669 195	1 615	0,1	2 455 075	92,0	178 505	6,7	34 000	1,3
Colombie–Britannique									
1951	1 165 210	727	0,1	1 112 937	95,5	39 433	3,4	12 113	1,0
1961	1 629 082	2 559	0,2	1 552 560	95,3	57 504	3,5	16 459	1,0
1971	2 184 625	1 775	0,1	2 054 690	94,1	101 435	4,6	26 725	1,2
1981	2 713 615	1 445	0,0	2 518 965	92,8	154 170	5,7	39 035	1,4
1991	3 247 510	1 140	0,0	2 976 330	91,6	207 175	6,4	62 865	1,9
1996	3 689 750	1 775	0,0	3 342 345	90,6	248 590	6,7	97 040	2,6
Yukon									
1951	9 096	10	0,1	8 337	91,7	519	5,7	230	2,5
1961	14 628	38	0,3	13 679	93,5	825	5,6	86	0,6
1971	18 390	10	0,0	17 130	93,1	1 210	6,6	40	0,2
1981	23 075	10	0,0	21 200	91,9	1 820	7,9	45	0,2
1991	27 655	25	0,1	25 035	90,5	2 570	9,3	25	0,1
1996	30 655	50	0,2	27 340	89,2	3 210	10,5	55	0,2

Tableau A.3
Population selon la connaissance des langues officielles, Canada, provinces, territoires et Canada moins le Québec, 1951 à 1996

Total		Connaissance des langues officielles							
		Français seulement		Anglais seulement		Français et anglais		Ni français, ni anglais	
		Effectif	%	Effectif	%	Effectif	%	Effectif	%
Territoires du Nord-Ouest									
1951	16 004	171	1,1	6 929	43,3	1 031	6,4	7 873	49,2
1961	22 998	109	0,5	13 554	58,9	1 614	7,0	7 721	33,6
1971	34 805	100	0,3	25 000	73,3	2 120	6,1	7 085	20,4
1981	45 545	60	0,1	36 385	79,9	2 755	6,0	6 435	13,9
1991	57 435	80	0,1	48 855	85,1	3 495	6,1	5 005	8,7
1996	64 125	40	0,6	55 880	87,1	4 035	6,3	4 170	6,5
Canada moins le Québec									
1951	9 953 748	207 570	2,1	8 924 582	89,7	689 317	6,9	132 279	1,3
1961	12 979 036	235 016	1,8	11 676 127	90,0	892 294	6,9	175 599	1,4
1971	15 540 545	211 240	1,4	13 837 025	89,0	1 236 365	8,0	255 915	1,6
1981	17 714 430	160 640	0,9	15 696 655	88,6	1 616 855	9,1	240 280	1,4
1991	20 183 735	151 370	0,7	17 733 005	87,9	1 985 670	9,8	313 690	1,6
1996	21 483 025	127 370	0,6	18 775 740	87,3	2 180 720	10,2	399 195	1,9

Nota : À partir du recensement de 1981, les effectifs ne comprennent pas les pensionnaires d'un établissement institutionnel. Ceux-ci représentent environ 1 p. cent de la population.

Sources : Statistique Canada, Recensement du Canada de 1951, 1961, 1971, 1981 1991 et 1996.

Tableau A.4
Population selon la première langue officielle parlée, Canada, provinces, territoires et Canada moins le Québec, 1991 et 1996

| | Total | Français | Anglais | Première langue officielle parlée | | Minorité de langue officielle.(1) | |
| | | | | Français et anglais | Ni français, ni anglais | | |
	Effectif	Effectif	Effectif	Effectif	Effectif	Effectif	%
Canada							
1991	26 994 035	6 704 675	19 709 370	217 080	362 910	6 813 220	25,2
1996	28 528 125	6 890 880	20 921 770	254 350	461 125	7 018 050	24,6
Terre–Neuve							
1991	563 940	2 630	560 485	95	725	2 675	0,5
1996	547 160	2 185	544 360	185	435	2 270	0,4
Île–du–Prince–Édouard							
1991	128 100	5 235	122 720	85	55	5 280	4,1
1996	132 855	5 270	127 425	120	30	5 335	4,0
Nouvelle–Écosse							
1991	890 950	35 470	853 680	835	970	35 885	4,0
1996	899 970	34 090	863 720	1 040	1 115	34 615	3,8
Nouveau–Brunswick							
1991	716 495	241 765	472 550	1 730	455	242 630	33,9
1996	729 630	240 060	487 200	1 965	405	241 040	33,0

Tableau A.4

Population selon la première langue officielle parlée, Canada, provinces, territoires et Canada moins le Québec, 1991 et 1996

	Total	Français	Anglais	Première langue officielle parlée Français et anglais	Ni français, ni anglais	Minorité de langue officielle (1)	
	Effectif	Effectif	Effectif	Effectif	Effectif	Effectif	%
Québec							
1991	6 810 300	5 772 180	832 045	144 505	61 565	904 305	13,3
1996	7 045 085	5 963 675	842 105	167 460	71 845	925 835	13,1
Ontario							
1991	9 977 050	483 445	9 255 865	52 410	185 335	509 650	5,1
1996	10 642 790	480 650	9 860 780	62 300	239 060	511 800	4,8
Manitoba							
1991	1 079 395	46 665	1 017 500	2 265	12 965	47 800	4,4
1996	1 100 290	45 570	1 041 230	2 010	11 490	46 570	4,2
Saskatchewan							
1991	976 040	19 315	950 350	975	5 395	19 805	2,0
1996	976 615	17 310	953 775	810	4 720	17 720	1,8
Alberta							
1991	2 519 180	50 565	2 433 560	5 430	29 635	53 280	2,1
1996	2 669 195	49 390	2 580 675	6 220	32 910	52 500	2,0

Tableau A.4
Population selon la première langue officielle parlée, Canada, provinces, territoires et Canada moins le Québec, 1991 et 1996

	Total	Première langue officielle parlée				Minorité de langue officielle(1)	
		Français	Anglais	Français et anglais	Ni français, ni anglais		
		Effectif	Effectif	Effectif	Effectif	Effectif	%
Colombie–Britannique							
1991	3 247 505	45 225	3 132 795	8 635	60 850	49 545	1,5
1996	3 689 755	50 285	3 532 485	12 040	94 945	56 310	1,5
Yukon							
1991	27 660	835	26 765	30	25	850	3,1
1996	30 655	1 080	29 455	70	45	1 115	3,6
Territoires du Nord-Ouest							
1991	57 435	1 345	51 055	90	4 935	1 390	2,4
1996	64 120	1 315	58 565	120	4 120	1 375	2,1
Canada moins le Québec							
1991	20 183 735	932 495	18 877 325	72 575	301 345	968 785	4,8
1996	21 483 040	927 205	20 079 665	86 890	389 280	970 650	4,5

(1) L'anglais est la première langue officielle parlée de la minorité de langue officielle du Québec, qui se compose de toutes les personnes ayant l'anglais en tant que première langue officielle parlée et de la moitié de celles ayant le français et l'anglais. Le français est la première langue officielle parlée de la minorité de langue officielle dans l'ensemble du pays et pour chaque province et territoire à l'extérieur du Québec, laquelle est formée de toutes les personnes ayant le français en tant que première langue officielle parlée et de la moitié de celles ayant le français et l'anglais.

Sources : Statistique Canada. Recensement de 1991 et 1996.

BON DE COMMANDE

Nom : ....

Adresse : ....

Téléphone : .... Télécopieur : ....

Couriel : ....

Programmes d'appui aux langues officielles, Patrimoine canadien
Ottawa (Ontario) K1A 0M5
Téléphone : (819) 994-2224 / Télécopieur : (819) 953-9353
Internet: http://www.pch.gc.ca/offlangoff/perspectives/index.htm

Veuillez cocher dans les cases appropriées le titre des textes désirés ainsi que la langue de votre choix.

☐ anglais   ☐ français   ☐ les deux

☐ Les langues au Canada / Languages in Canada

☐ Lois linguistiques du Canada annotées (Lois constitutionnelles, fédérales, provinciales et territoriales) / Annotated Language Laws of Canada (Constitutional, Federal, Provincial and Territorial)

☐ Langue et bilinguisme : les approches économiques /
Economic Approaches to Language and Bilingualism

☐ Langues officielles au Canada : transformer le paysage linguistique /
Official Languages in Canada: Changing the Language Landscape (bilingual)

☐ Le dynamisme socio-économique des communautés de langue officielle /
The Socio-Economic Vitality of Official Language Communities

☐ Droits à l'instruction dans la langue de la minorité : état de la situation /
Status Report: Minority-Language Educational Rights (bilingual)

☐ Les liens dans la francophonie canadienne (bilingue) /
Francophones in Canada: A Community of Interests (bilingual)